Expansion or Exodus: Why Do Russian Corporations Invest Abroad?

Expansion or Exodus: Why Do Russian Corporations Invest Abroad? has been co-published simultaneously as *Journal of East-West Business,* Volume 11, Numbers 3/4 2005.

Expansion or Exodus: Why Do Russian Corporations Invest Abroad?

Kari Liuhto, PhD
Editor

Expansion or Exodus: Why Do Russian Corporations Invest Abroad? has been co-published simultaneously as *Journal of East-West Business,* Volume 11, Numbers 3/4 2005.

Routledge
Taylor & Francis Group
New York London

First published by

The International Business Press®, 10 Alice Street, Binghamton, NY 13904-1580 USA

The International Business Press® is an imprint of The Haworth Press, Inc., 10 Alice Street, Binghamton, NY 13904-1580 USA.

This edition published 2012 by Routledge

Routledge
Taylor & Francis Group
711 Third Avenue
New York, NY 10017

Routledge
Taylor & Francis Group
2 Park Square, Milton Park
Abingdon, Oxon OX14 4RN

Expansion or Exodus: Why Do Russian Corporations Invest Abroad? has been co-published simultaneously as *Journal of East-West Business*™, Volume 11, Numbers 3/4 2005.

Cover design by Lora Wiggins

Library of Congress Cataloging-in-Publication Data

Expansion or exodus : why do Russian corporations invest abroad? / Kari Liuhto, editor.
p. cm.
"Expansion or exodus : why do Russian corporations invest abroad? has been co-published simultaneously as Journal of East-West Business, Volume 11, Numbers 3/4 2005."
Includes bibliographical references and index.
ISBN-13: 978-0-7890-3285-0 (alk. paper)
ISBN-10: 0-7890-3285-6 (alk. paper)
ISBN-13: 978-0-7890-3286-7 (soft cover : alk. paper)
ISBN-10: 0-7890-3286-4 (soft cover : alk. paper)
1. Investments, Russian. 2. Russia (Federation)–Commerce. 3. Corporations–Russia (Federation) I. Liuhto, Kari II. Journal of East-West business. v. 11, no. 3/4, 2005 (Special issue)

HF3630.2.Z5E96 2006
332.67'347--dc22

2006000743

Expansion or Exodus: Why Do Russian Corporations Invest Abroad?

CONTENTS

ABOUT THE EDITOR

Kari Liuhto, PhD, holds a professorship in international business at the Turku School of Economics and Business Administration. Liuhto concentrates his research activities on the energy sector in Russia, wider Europe-related economic affairs, foreign direct investment flows into/from transition economies, and enterprise restructuring in the ex-Soviet Union. Liuhto is the director of the Pan-European Institute.

Foreword

After the collapse of the USSR, the activities of the Russian firms abroad have increased. The Russian companies have invested USD 50-70 billion outside the country. The majority of the FDI outflow has taken place during this millennium. When evaluating the total amount of the Russian capital abroad, one needs to keep in mind that recorded FDI forms only a tip of the iceberg, i.e., it does not include the giant capital flight from Russia. According to the European Commission, the Russian capital flight was USD 250 billion during 1992-2002, i.e., the Russian capital abroad totals some USD 300 billion.[1]

Although some of the Russian money has returned home via Cyprus and some other countries, most of it has remained abroad. Russia's modest inward FDI stock worth USD 53 billion supports the above conclusion. Besides, one should not forget that the home-returning money forms less than a third of the Russian inward stock, Cyprus being so far the major source of the Russian capital round tripping.[2] The recent EU membership of Cyprus may, however, move the Russian investment transit to some other location.

The statistics draw an unclear picture where the Russian investments have ended. The UN-based statistics indicate that Russian capital has arrived especially in the EU and the USA. The enterprise databank of the Pan-European Institute reveals that the Russian companies are strengthening their presence, especially in the former USSR. As many of the CIS economies are small and politically fragile, the role of the Russian firms becomes emphasized there.

As the Russian oil companies and natural gas giant, Gazprom, are behind the majority of the Russian capital abroad, the ex-socialist countries have become frightened that the Russian Government uses energy

[Haworth co-indexing entry note]: "Foreword." Co-published simultaneously in *Journal of East-West Business* (The Haworth Press, Inc.) Vol. 11, No. 3/4, 2005, pp. xxv-xxvi; and: *Expansion or Exodus: Why Do Russian Corporations Invest Abroad?* (ed: Kari Liuhto) The Haworth Press, Inc., 2005, pp. xiii-xiv. Single or multiple copies of this article are available for a fee from The Haworth Document Delivery Service [1-800-HAWORTH, 9:00 a.m. - 5:00 p.m. (EST). E-mail address: docdelivery@haworthpress.com].

Available online at http://www.haworthpress.com/web/JEB

companies as tools of its foreign policy to keep the ex-Soviet republics in Russia's sphere of interest. In some cases these fears are grounded but one needs to bear in mind that the outward expansion of the Russian firms is becoming less politically-motivated, as non-energy-related companies have also begun their internationalization.

When evaluating the overall impact of the Russian business expansion abroad, one should keep in mind that the trade rapprochement via Russia's WTO membership is not a sufficient condition in integrating Russia closer to the world economy, and hence more emphasis should be placed on the investment integration. The need for integrating Russia closer to the world economy grows, particularly in times when the authoritarian and chauvinistic views are lifting their head in the country.

This volume dedicated to the outward expansion of the Russian businesses starts with a global view on the Russian companies abroad. Thereafter, the operations of the Russian firms in old, new and forthcoming EU member states are described. In addition to the country-analyses, some company cases are presented.

I gratefully acknowledge the financial support obtained from the Finnish Ministry of Education, the Academy of Finland and various research foundations. Without their financial aid, it would not have been possible to conduct the research work at its current extent.

NOTES

1. The Russian GDP measured at market prices was some USD 550 billion in 2004.
2. Cyprus, representing a fifth of Russia's total inward FDI stock, is the largest investor country to Russia.

Kari Liuhto
Director
Pan-European Institute
www.tukkk.fi/pei/e

Introduction

Since the collapse of the former Soviet Union, tremendous changes and developments have taken place in the new Russian Federation as well as its trade relationship with other countries, in particular with her so-called former allies. Among all, performance and growth of Russian corporations has been phenomenal. It is expected that their performance will increase at an accelerating rate in the years to come, especially when Russian Federation become a member of the World Trade Organization (WTO) in the near future. Professor Kari Liuhto, Director of the Pan-European Institute of the Turku School of Economics and Business Administration, is to be congratulated for bringing this project to fruition. This volume is a welcome addition to a growing body of knowledge in this emerging subject area.

Since the start of the transition from a centrally planned to a market economy, the Russian Federation has always been a large net capital exporter country as its FDI outflows have exceeded its FDI inflows. In the 1990s, most of the outflows were of an informal nature, and unregistered in the balance of payments, or mis-registered under other items. Since 2003, their recording has improved. Using the FDI inflows, the registered FDI outflows and the estimated total FDI-type capital abroad for 1993-2004 derived from those improved data, the Russian Federation shows the signs of a major source country of outward FDI.

The article by Kálmán Kalotay asks the question how can a lower-middle income country become a net capital exporter. This is a major unexplained anomaly for the Heckscher-Ohlin-Samuelson paradigm of international trade and the investment-development path paradigm of international investment. The seemingly large Russian paradox could be resolved by two ways: bringing the analysis of the business and eco-

[Haworth co-indexing entry note]: "Introduction." Kaynak, Erdener. Co-published simultaneously in *Journal of East-West Business* (The Haworth Press, Inc.) Vol. 11, No. 3/4, 2005, pp. 1-8; and: *Expansion or Exodus: Why Do Russian Corporations Invest Abroad?* (ed: Kari Liuhto) The Haworth Press, Inc., 2005, pp. 1-8. Single or multiple copies of this article are available for a fee from The Haworth Document Delivery Service [1-800-HAWORTH, 9:00 a.m. - 5:00 p.m. (EST). E-mail address: docdelivery@haworthpress.com].

Available online at http://www.haworthpress.com/web/JEB

doi:10.1300/J097v11n03_01

nomic environment–still difficult–into the analysis of international investment position, or bringing the duality of the Russian economy and society as an explanatory factor into the picture. 'Duality' means the co-existence of two radically different economies and societies within the boundaries of the Russian Federation: the majority of society and economy is indeed lower middle income (or even low income) and is short of capital; but there is a capital- and resource-rich segment of society and economy–the 'oligarchy' created under the presidency of Boris Yeltsyn (1991-1999) controlling large parts of the privatized natural resources of the country and behaving like a high-income country.

This dualism creates two interrelated problems: one of them is that the excess capital of the resource-rich segment does not necessarily target the poor segment of the society but rather foreign locations as Russian firms desire to control the value chain of their natural resources globally. Another related problem is that in the medium and longer term, this situation may create too many social tensions and becomes unsustainable. That may in part explain why the action by the Government has targeted one of the leading outward investing firms. Nevertheless, with the political changes currently taking place, only a limited increase in the influence of the State is expected to happen. The most probably scenario for the future is that Russian TNCs will only marginally modify their expansion abroad. They may also end up reflecting more foreign policy considerations than before. It is also expected that in the future the behaviour of Russian firms will more and more approach the behaviour of other global firms, located in developed countries.

According to Vahtra and Liuhto, until recently, the growth of the Russian outward foreign direct investments has largely relied on the natural resource-based companies, and the oil and gas companies in particular. In recent years, also the Russian manufacturing and ICT companies have started their expansion abroad. The improved financial situation of the companies has brought along the interest towards more demanding internationalization modes, and more careful selection process of the foreign ventures. The policy measures that support the integration of Russian companies into the world markets through outward expansion are the fastest means to improve Russian competitiveness abroad.

The Russian leading oil, gas, and metal companies already rank among the world's most prominent actors in their respective fields. Although the exports and foreign sales promotion currently remain the most common modes of internationalization of the Russian companies, many of the firms are already engaged in more demanding foreign operational modes. Several of the companies other than the natural resource-based companies have already shown the way in employing competitive internationalization practices.

The Russian companies often play different games in different regions. The internationalization of the Russian companies often pursues political ambitions of the Russian Government in Russia's neighboring countries, whereas the expansion towards the Western markets more often embodies economic motives. Pursuing transparent and non-politically motivated investments abroad, the Russian firms would face a completely different attitude milieu in the recipient countries. From the host countries' viewpoint, the investments by giant Russian oil, gas, and electricity conglomerates are often puzzling through their widespread influence in given sector in a particular host country. In case the Russian Government's policies towards the outward internationalisation of the companies become less politically-oriented, the foreign investments guided by economic rationality are likely to increase. The revival of Russian manufacturing and telecom sectors, for instance, further advances the non-politically motivated investments from Russia.

Analyzing the motives of Russian investments in Germany, the article by Andreas Heinrich identifies the following: (1) for market seeking purposes several Russian corporations have established representative offices or marketing subsidiaries in Germany; (2) market seeking in combination with strategic asset or capability seeking through joint ventures and acquisitions can be determined as the other main motive for the internationalization of Russian companies and their investment activities in Germany; (3) capability seeking through co-operation agreements or strategic partnerships also provide impetus for the internationalization of Russian firms in Germany; and (4) stability seeking (through capital flight) is also an important motive.

As an old EU member state, Germany's reluctance to host Russian investments is much milder than in the new member countries due to different historical experiences. Since the mid-1970s, the Soviet Union (and later the Russian Federation) has established itself as a reliable trading partner of strategic important energy sources, primarily natural gas.

However, there arc somc basic difficulties for other Russian companies in acquiring stakes in German or–more generally–in companies in old EU member states. Markets are highly competitive and dominated by capital-scraping western companies and, therefore, lucrative acquisitions often require much more capital than privatization auctions can generate in Central and Eastern Europe. Additionally, Russian companies do not–at least not in an unknown business environment–have the competitive edge.

Another reason for limited Russian presence in Germany may lie in the nature of the structure of the internationalizing companies. The Russian economy is dominated by the raw materials sector, as are the trade and outward FDI structures. Oil and gas companies dominate the internationalization of Russian firms followed by companies from the metals sector. The motives for the internationalization of Russian companies in the raw materials sector are more resource seeking than market seeking. Therefore, these companies have established mostly only representational offices in Germany to foster their exports.

Nevertheless, Russian machinery, automotive and financial corporations as well as food and glass producers and IT companies have notably expanded their international operations during the past few years. These companies provide an example of an active market-seeking strategy. However, only a small number of Russian corporations is involved in more specific investments in Germany, driven by the motivation of strategic asset and capability seeking.

Small businesses seem to dominate the investment activities in number in Germany. Larger, export-orientated Russian companies use Germany as an entry to Europe–primarily to the old EU member states–by using its technological and intellectual infrastructure.

The paper by Kilvits, Purju and Pädam analyses volume, structure and role of Russia's FDIs in the Baltic States. Russia's FDI in the Baltic States has been increasing over the last two to three years. The EU membership of the Baltic States and access to the EU market, accompanied by available sources for investment as a result of economic growth in Russia have been the main reasons for that increase.

The primary energy resources and raw materials from Russia are important for the Baltic States. The investments that accompany and support that trade could be a reasonable economic step. At the same time, FDI from Russia have been met with suspicion in the Baltic States. The two main reasons for trying to avoid Russian investments have been the fear of losing control over the vital aspects of the economy and sometimes an unclear source of investments.

The share of Russia's foreign direct investment stock was 5.4% in Latvia, 6.0% in Lithuania and 1.2% in Estonia of the total stock of FDI. These figures suggest a low penetration rate of Russian foreign direct investments in the Baltic countries. According to indirect estimates, the amount of FDI with Russia's background is larger, up to 3-4 times the official figures.

Russia's outward foreign direct investments concern mostly large enterprises in the sector of natural resources and transportation. This structure is detectable also in the Baltic economies, as Russian investments to a substantial degree comprise investments into the energy sector and transit shipment infrastructure.

The paper ends with a case study of the natural gas transportation and distribution company Eesti Gaas. The gas companies in the Baltic States and Finland are one example of FDI from Russia. The main supplier, Gasprom, has been a minor shareholder together with a large international Western company, providing know-how, financial resources for restructuring and access to already existing or perspective networks.

The Russian investor has acted as a business partner in the case of Eesti Gaas, which can be explained by different circumstances. Gazprom's corporate culture is business oriented. Estonia does not have a strategic role in the gas market. The supplies to Estonia are not vulnerable to short-term interruptions in supplies from Russia due to the underground natural gas storage in Incukalns, Latvia.

Russia's FDI into the Baltic States can be considered as a feature of internationalisation of economies in the Baltic Sea region. A possible linkage to power politics and government interventions through FDI depends on the future political and economic developments in the region, Russia's development being the main factor.

Oil refining is Lithuania's third largest sector within the country's processing industry. In 2000, it represented more than 9% of the Lithuanian GDP. Mazeikiu Nafta is an oil refining and transporting company. Mazeikiu Nafta paid almost 11% of whole excise tax collected by the Lithuanian Government in 1996 whilst in 2002 MN's excise tax contribution reached 55% of the whole excise collections.

The research by Tvaronaviciene and Saee aims at elaborating performance of an oil refinery owned by a Russian corporation in Lithuania. This case study illustrates the importance of foreign direct investment, namely Russian FDI for Lithuanian economic development. The authors strive to trace how important Russian capital is for the Lithuanian oil business. The study examines the development of the oil refinery: (1) from its initial state-ownership to (2) privatization conducted by an American private company and, finally (3) to its acquisition with the Russian capital.

Poland is one of the biggest FDI host countries in CEE and therefore should be a natural market for Russia's biggest companies, especially for its oil producers. However, the share of Russian oil in the Polish energy market is marginal. In the study of Małgorzata Runiewicz, Lukoil's impact on the business expansion and Polish economy is examined and its impact was found to be rather limited and could be described as the direct and the indirect one.

The direct impact on the energy sector and the whole economy can be regarded as rather positive. The company has contributed to:

- capital formation, stimulation of Polish exports of petroleum products,
- decreased the growing deficit in the Polish current account in the relations with Russia (Poland has largest trade deficit with Russia),
- guarantees for long-term supplies of unprocessed fuels from Russia,
- stimulated a long-term sustainable economic development, by implementing environmentally friendly production technologies,
- has a very clear investment development plan for Poland.

The indirect negative impact of the Lukoil investment in Poland results from the corruption and political involvement related to the expansion of the Russian investments in the strategic assets (e.g., Lukoil's participation in the privatization of the Gdansk Refinery).

The EU enlargement opens new business opportunities for the Russian companies and their investments in the energy sector. It is expected that Russia's aim to become a member of the World Trade Organization will increase its credibility as a business partner and contribute to an increase of the Russian direct investments in the region.

In order to improve the investment climate, contribute from Russian capital and enable the Lukoil's company expansion the Polish government bodies should designate the target or prioritized areas for the Lukoil investments. The latter will require introduction of necessary managerial or fiscal incentives. One of the key priorities could be the environmentally friendly projects, energy infrastructure development and R&D activities.

Transpetrol was founded to manage the Czechoslovak section of the Druzhba pipeline system built in the 1960s to connect the USSR with Eastern Europe. With the breakup of Czechoslovakia, the Slovak section retained the original name and became the sole operator of the national oil pipeline system of the Slovak Republic. Due to the exceptional importance of petroleum transfer and storage for the Slovak economy, Transpetrol was categorized as a strategic enterprise and remained 100% state owned. In 2000, the Slovak Government decided to partially privatize Transpetrol. The winner of the auction was the Russian company Yukos, which gained 49% of the shares in Transpetrol and became a strategic partner in the further development of Transpetrol's business.

It was pointed out by Viera Pochybova that the arrival of the strategic investor was welcomed because it was expected that it could solve some of the problems that Transpetrol was facing at that time. However, despite the fact that Yukos started some promising projects in Transpetrol, its activities were hampered after the Russian company was accused of tax frauds and was charged billions of dollars in back taxes. It was only a question of time when the problems at Yukos start to have impact on the Slovak company. The bankruptcy of the Russian company could affect the whole Slovak energy sector.

The Slovak government has started recently to take measures to regain the 49% stake in Transpetrol. Nevertheless, the success of the proceeding negotiations depends largely on the willingness of the Russian side as Transpetrol's stake was arrested as a part of Yukos' property and its future can be determined only through cooperation with the Russian Government.

The Slovak Government also faces another barrier–it can lose the majority stake in Transpetrol because of the decision of the Court of the Slovakian town Prešov, which decided that 34% of Transpetrol shares out of 51% that belong to the government belong to a local businessman and his firm.

Thus there are many hesitations about the future development of Transpetrol. The loss of the control over the company threatens the national security and would be the worst possible scenario. However, there are more different possibilities what could happen. Transpetrol is a company of strategic importance for Slovakia. Its future, which is quite blurred at the moment due to the recent events, will have a substantial impact on the development of Slovak economy.

If serious problems of business ethics continue to plague the way business is conducted within Russia, the internationalization of Russian companies puts forward the question if they bring along and utilize their domestic business culture when operating abroad or try and adopt to higher standards corporate culture and business ethics.

Lukoil Bulgaria and Lukoil Neftochim Bourgas oil refinery are one of the biggest and most important economic players in the Bulgarian economy. The importance of Neftochim for the Bulgarian economy could be described with two figures: the oil refinery produces 9% of Bulgaria GDP and accounts for 25% of all taxes collected by the Bulgarian government.

The paper by Peter Zashev reviews what patterns of business culture and corporate governance Lukoil demonstrated in Bulgaria against what could be perceived the negative side of the Russian business culture.

The business cultural influence of foreign investors is a subject that is still relatively unexplored by the cross-cultural management discipline. The main problem is how that influence could be qualified and quantified. In the absence of an established methodological instrument for measuring the cultural influence of an international investor the author employs a framework suggested by McCarthy and Puffer and somewhat modified for the analysis of the Russian corporate governance.

The secondary data collected and presented in the article conclude that Lukoil Bulgaria is an example of a Russian investor who tries to be a role model and that is an ambition that should be only encouraged. In future refining the theoretical model and using primary data such as questionnaires and interviews could considerably improve the quality of the research.

The paper by Lisitsyn et al. describes outward internationalization of Russian leading mobile operator Mobile TeleSystems (MTS). Foreign market expansion of the company under review was preceded by growth within the national boundaries. Hence the article starts with a brief overview of the Russian cellular market and its main actors.

The first company's foreign market entry occurred in 2002. From the very beginning MTS focused on the CIS states. That outward internationalization policy was based on the economic and political ties inherited from the Soviet past. Relatively low penetration rate and rapidly increasing subscriber base provided significant opportunities on target markets. Knowledge of business environment of the CIS countries, quite similar to that in Russia, favored the company's internationalization.

The sequence of external market entries was determined by the maturity of the cellular sectors and the level of infrastructure development. The company started with Belarus and Ukraine in 2002. Later it entered less developed but promising markets of Uzbekistan and Turkmenistan. The paper depicts managerial practices of the company used for the entries. In terms of general entry mode the company mostly acquired existing mobile operators. But the managerial approach was specific for each entry. The company demonstrated its ability to build positive relationships with the authorities in the target countries and to overcome successfully the administrative barriers. That was an issue of utmost importance for the company as the markets under review were strictly regulated by the state. Thus the article gives the example of successful expansion management within the framework of the post-Soviet economic environment.

Erdener Kaynak

Outward Foreign Direct Investment from Russia in a Global Context

Kálmán Kalotay

SUMMARY. Since the beginning of the transition from centrally planned to market economy, the FDI outflows of the Russian Federation have consistently exceeded the inflows. In the 1990s, most of the outflows were of an informal nature, and unregistered in the balance of payments, or misregistered under other items. Since 2003, their recording has improved. However, the question remains: how can a lower-middle income country become a net capital exporter? It is supposed to be the combined result of economic and political factors such as the economic and business environment, still deemed to be difficult. The fact that the 'oligarchy' created under the presidency of Boris Yeltsin (1991-1999) continues to control large parts of the privatized natural resources of the country also stimulated capital exporting behavior. With the political changes currently taking place, only a limited increase in the influence of the State is expected to happen. Moreover, the strategic interest of Russian firms to control their vertical value chains through outward FDI is expected to remain in the longer term. *[Article copies available for a fee from The Haworth Document Delivery Service: 1-800-HAWORTH. E-mail address: <docdelivery@haworthpress.com> Website: <http://www.HaworthPress.com> © 2005 by The Haworth Press, Inc. All rights reserved.]*

Kálmán Kalotay is Economic Affairs Officer, United Nations Conference on Trade and Development, Geneva, Switzerland.

The views in this article are those of the author and do not necessarily reflect the opinion of the United Nations.

[Haworth co-indexing entry note]: "Outward Foreign Direct Investment from Russia in a Global Context." Kalotay, Kálmán. Co-published simultaneously in *Journal of East-West Business* (The Haworth Press, Inc.) Vol. 11, No. 3/4, 2005, pp. 9-22; and: *Expansion or Exodus: Why Do Russian Corporations Invest Abroad?* (ed: Kari Liuhto) The Haworth Press, Inc., 2005, pp. 9-22. Single or multiple copies of this article are available for a fee from The Haworth Document Delivery Service [1-800-HAWORTH, 9:00 a.m. - 5:00 p.m. (EST). E-mail address: docdelivery@haworthpress.com].

Available online at http://www.haworthpress.com/web/JEB

doi:10.1300/J097v11n03_02

KEYWORDS. Outward direct investment, Russia

A GLOBAL PLAYER

Since the start of transition from centrally planned to market economy, the Russian Federation has always been a large net capital exporter country (its FDI outflows have exceeded its FDI inflows). Until recently, this observation was based on deductions from existing information and estimates (see Bulatov, 1998, for a summary) as the official statistics of the country used to register only a fraction of the real outflows of the private sector.

With recent improvements in the data collection and reporting of the Central Bank of Russia, it is now also possible to confirm the accuracy of previously made estimates. The cumulative amount of 'net capital outflow by non-financial enterprises and households' for the period January 1994-September 2004 (USD 167 bn) is by and large in line with earlier estimates for the 'unregistered' or 'misregistered' FDI outflows of the country. For example, Bulatov (1998) has suggested that a figure of USD 20 billion to USD 30 billion would have been more realistic estimate for Russian FDI outward stocks already in 1997. In the same vein, UNCTAD (2002, 84) estimated the 'capital flight' from the Russian Federation over the 1990s to be in excess of USD 20 billion per year. In the light of statistics gathered at a later stage, this amount proved to be right for various years (e.g., 1996, 1997 and 2000).

The reasons why data collection needed to undergo major improvements included the problems with capturing fully the value of assets accumulated by the Soviet Union abroad or inherited by the Russian Federation in other former Soviet republics and the tendency of Russian firms to finance their foreign expansion through outflows registered under other flows (such as portfolio flows, trade finance or service payments), increasing the whole outward FDI stock substantially (Bulatov, 1998). In this respect, Russian 'capital flight' has not been 'classical' in the sense that it could not be proxied by the usual methods focusing on the 'errors and omissions' item of the balance of payments (Claessens and Naude, 1993).

Plotting the FDI inflows, the registered FDI outflows and the estimated total FDI-type capital abroad for 1993-2004, the Russian Federation shows the signs of a major source country of outward FDI. But the official and estimated outward FDI data give somewhat different signals. If only the officially registered FDI outflow is considered against the FDI inflows, there is a gradual shift towards a net capital exporting status (Figure 1). Indeed, since 2002, FDI outflows exceed the FDI inflows. If the 'assumed' FDI outflows are considered, the country has been a major capital exporter since the mid-1990s. The value of these outflows fluctuates sharply, and seems to decline after 2000, reflecting the efforts of authorities to slow down and regularize the 'spontaneous' outflows of FDI.

These data indicate that, in global comparison, the Russian Federation is a major source country of outward FDI. If the official outward FDI stock of 2003 (USD 72 billion) is considered, the Russian Federation is already among the 20 most important source countries of the world, accounting for almost one per cent of the global stock (Table 1).

This value is higher than that of a number of small high-income countries (e.g., Finland, Austria, Norway, Portugal) and that of the majority

FIGURE 1. FDI Inflows, FDI Outflows, and 'Net Capital Outflows' of the Russian Federation, 1993-2004 (USD Billion)

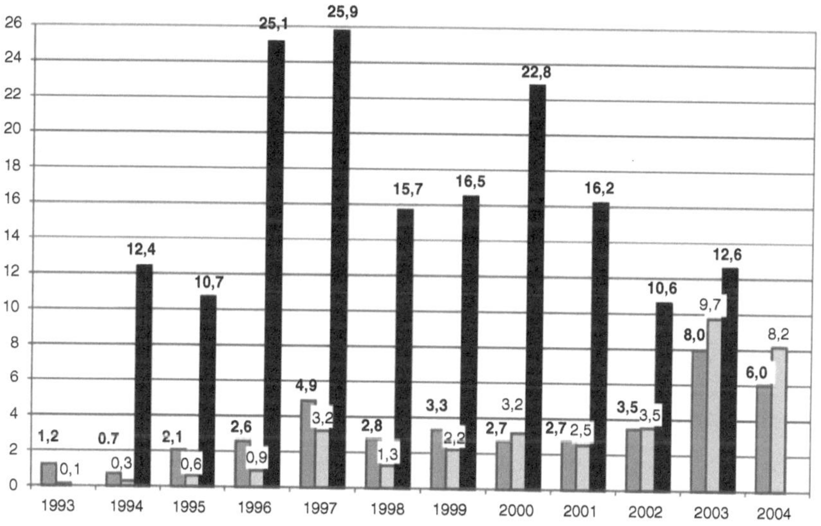

Left column = FDI inflow
Middle column = FDI outflow
Right column = net capital outflow

Note: Projection for 2004 is based on three-quarter data.

Sources UNCTAD, FDI/TNC database (*http://stats.unctad.org/fdi/*), data provided by the Central Bank of Russia, and the author's estimates.

TABLE 1. The World League Table of Outward FDI Stock, 2003 (USD Billion)

Rank	Economy	Income group	Value	Share
	World		8,217.3	100.0%
1	United States	High	2,069.0	25.2%
2	United Kingdom	High	1,128.6	13.7%
3	France	High	643.4	7.8%
4	Germany	High	622.5	7.6%
5	Netherlands	High	384.4	4.7%
6	Switzerland	High	344.1	4.2%
7	Hong Kong, China	High	336.1	4.1%
8	Japan	High	335.5	4.1%
9	Belgium and Luxembourg	High	334.1	4.1%
10	Canada	High	307.9	3.7%
11	Italy	High	238.9	2.9%
12	Spain	High	207.5	2.5%
13	Sweden	High	189.3	2.3%
...	**Russian Federation (all outflows)**	**Lower middle**	**168.5**	**2.0%**
14	Australia	High	117.1	1.4%
15	Singapore	High	90.9	1.1%
16	Denmark	High	77.1	0.9%
17	**Russian Federation**	**Lower middle**	**72.3**	**0.9%**
18	Finland	High	68.7	0.8%
19	Taiwan Province of China	High	65.2	0.8%
20	Austria	High	59.1	0.7%
21	Brazil	Lower middle	54.6	0.7%
22	Norway	High	40.6	0.5%
23	Portugal	High	38.5	0.5%
24	China	Lower middle	37.0	0.5%
25	Korea, Republic of	High	34.5	0.4%
...				
44	Turkey	Lower middle	5.5	0.1%
45	India	Low	5.1	0.1%
...				
51	Hungary	Upper middle	3.9	0.05%
61	Poland	Upper middle	1.8	0.02%
62	Slovenia	High	1.8	0.02%
63	Czech Republic	Upper middle	1.7	0.02%

Sources: UNCTAD, FDI/TNC database (*http://stats.unctad.org/fdi/*) and the Central Bank of the Russian Federation.

of emerging economies. In the emerging economy group, only the outward FDI stock of Hong Kong (China) and Singapore exceed that of the Russian Federation. Other leading emerging economies that are usually reported as new outward FDI powerhouses (e.g., Taiwan Province of China, Brazil, China, Republic of Korea, Turkey and India), all fall behind the Russian Federation. Moreover, the outward FDI stock of the new EU member countries such as Hungary, Poland, Slovenia and the Czech Republic are by degrees smaller. If all the capital outflows of the enterprise sector of the Russian Federation as reported by the Central Bank had been counted (USD 169 billion until the end of 2003), the Russian Federation would advance to the 14th position worldwide, ahead of Singapore.

THE RUSSIAN OUTWARD FDI PARADOX

The presence of the lower-middle income Russian Federation in the global top list of outward FDI is a major unexplained anomaly for the standard theories of international trade and investment: the Heckscher-Ohlin-Samuelson (HOS) paradigm (Heckscher, 1919; Ohlin, 1933; Samuelson, 1948, 1949) and the investment-development path (IDP; Dunning, 1981, 1986). For the HOS paradigm, the Russian exception is the biggest challenge since the Leontief paradox (Leontief, 1954; according to which the United States exported labor-intensive goods and imported capital intensive goods). For the IDP, the behavior of the net investment position is completely the opposite to what the theory would predict: instead of inward FDI exceeding outward FDI and growing faster than the latter, outward FDI exceeds inward FDI and grows faster than inward FDI.

In the list of the 20 largest source countries of outward FDI, the Russian Federation is the only lower-middle income country. It is in the company of 19 high-income countries that typically have a GDP per capita of 10 to 20 times higher than the Russian Federation (Table 1). The next lower-income countries on the list are Brazil (21st) and China (24th), the two giants of the developing world. If the Russian Federation is put into its own peer group of 20 major lower middle-income countries, it behaves like an outlier, following the patterns of high-income countries (Table 2).

The group as a whole follows the predictions of the HOS and IDP paradigms, with an average net inward FDI position of more than 2% of GDP. In addition to the Russian Federation, there are only two coun-

TABLE 2. Net Outward FDI per GDP in Selected Lower Middle-Income Countries, Average of 1999-2003 (%)

Country	Net outward FDI per GDP	Outward FDI per GDP	Inward FDI per GDP
Russian Federation	*4.40%*	*5.69%*	*1.29%*
(Based on the net capital outflow by non-financial enterprises)			
Indonesia	1.41%	0.07%	−1.33%
Iran, Islamic Rep.	1.05%	1.14%	0.09%
Russian Federation	*0.00%*	*1.29%*	*1.29%*
(Based on officially registered outward FDI)			
Turkey	−0.51%	0.29%	0.79%
Egypt	−0.76%	0.03%	0.79%
Algeria	−1.32%	0.07%	1.39%
Philippines	−1.65%	−0.03%	1.62%
Belarus	−1.90%	−0.28%	1.62%
Colombia	−1.96%	0.56%	2.52%
Ukraine	−1.99%	0.02%	2.01%
South Africa	−2.05%	−0.26%	1.79%
Thailand	−2.45%	0.18%	2.62%
Peru	−2.60%	0.10%	2.70%
Romania	−2.72%	0.02%	2.74%
Morocco	−3.45%	0.12%	3.57%
China	−3.72%	0.24%	3.96%
Brazil	−4.00%	0.17%	4.17%
Macedonia, FYR	−4.53%	0.01%	4.53%
Kazakhstan	−8.95%	0.25%	9.20%
Azerbaijan	−11.52%	5.69%	17.20%
Weighted sample average 1	**−2.49%**	**0.33%**	**2.82%**
(Based on officially registered outward FDI)			
Weighted sample average 2	**−2.12%**	**0.70%**	**2.82%**
(Based on the net capital outflow by non-financial enterprises)			

Sources: UNCTAD, FDI/TNC database (*http://stats.unctad.org/fdi/*), data provided by the Bank of Russia, and the author's estimates.

tries, namely Indonesia and the Islamic Republic of Iran, that are net capital exporting.[1] However, if the total outflow of capital from the Russian Federation is counted, the net outward position reaches more than 4% of GDP. On the other extreme, the other oil producing countries of the former Soviet Union (Azerbaijan and Kazakhstan) reach very high levels of net inward FDI position per GDP, and even the ratio in China and Brazil is around 4% of GDP–in favor of inward FDI.

EXPLANATIONS OF THE OUTWARD FDI PARADOX

The seemingly large paradox of the Russian Federation for the HOS and IDP theories could be resolved by two ways: bringing the analysis of the business and economic environment into the analysis of international investment position, or bringing the duality of the Russian economy and society as an explanatory factor into the picture.

The Russian Business Environment

One possibility is to bring the analysis of the business and economic environment into the analysis of international investment position. We have to assume that, *ceteris paribus*, the more difficult such an environment is the more the net investment position is shifting toward outward FDI. This analysis also has to consider the fact that countries with relatively difficult business and economic environments, say China or India, have alternative ways to improve the situation of foreign and domestic investors, through either creating special economic zones or other mechanism establishing pockets of better business environment. In the Russian Federation, the business environment is still difficult, despite recent improvements, and the alternative ways of creating areas of better treatment do not seem to work efficiently. Indeed, the recent changes of the business environment have sent contradictory messages to domestic and foreign investors. On the one hand, there have been a series of impressive measures to improve the Russian business climate including the rationalization of taxes. On the other hand, in the case of Yukos, tax administration has been used to reach certain non-economic, non-fiscal goals. At the moment the tax authority approached, in November 2004, a joint venture with a foreign investor (TNK-BP), it sent the message that a potential reversal of the improvement of the business climate was not totally excluded, despite the fact that the amount requested (USD 90 million) was a fraction of the one demanded from Yukos (USD 3.5 billion for year 2001 only) (Ostrovsky, 2004).

The Duality of Russian Economy and Society

Another possibility to explain the Russian paradox is to assume that there are two radically different economies and societies within the boundaries of the Russian Federation: the majority of society and the economy is indeed lower middle income (or even low income) and is short of capital; but there is a capital- and resource-rich segment of society and economy that behaves like a high-income country. This dualism creates two interrelated problems: one of them is that the excess capital of the resource-rich segment does not necessarily target the poor segment of the society but rather foreign locations. Another related problem is that in the medium and longer term, this situation may create too many social tensions and becomes unsustainable. That may in part explain why the action by the government has targeted one of the leading outward investing firms.

Outward FDI by Russian firms is motivated partly by a desire to control the value chain of natural resources globally (like in the case of Norilsk Nickel's investment into South Africa's Gold Fields). Data for the top 25 transnational corporations (TNCs) of Central and Eastern Europe in 2000 (UNCTAD, 2002) confirm that Russian TNCs for which data are available are globally spread. In 2000, the network spreads index (the number of foreign locations is which the firm is present divided by the number of foreign countries of the world) stood at more than 5% for Russian firms, as compared to around 3% for other Central and Eastern European firms (*idem*). Within the strategy of global reach, Russian companies continue to focus a large part of their outward FDI in other member countries of the Commonwealth of Independent States (CIS). In 2002-2003, four of the 10 top destinations of outward FDI projects from the Russian Federation were other CIS member countries.

In 2002-2003, the majority (8 of the 15: Lukoil, Gazprom, Yukos, Group Alliance, Itera Group, Rosneft, RusAl, Alrosa) of the leading Russian outward investing firms–in terms of new projects started abroad–were natural-resource-based groups. In 2004, one has to add Norilsk Nickel, Russia's biggest mining company, which bought a 20% stake in Gold Fields Ltd. (South Africa) for USD 1.2 billion as it diversified to gold output to complement its already existing production of nickel and palladium. The transaction made Norilsk the world's fourth-biggest gold miner overnight.

Russian natural-resource-based firms started internationalizing through exporting their products. The profitability of those exports benefited from the difference in price levels between the domestic and world markets. As a next step, to diversify the production basis and to access foreign markets, Russian energy companies started acquiring companies abroad and establishing foreign affiliates. These affiliates are also used as a means to avoid excessive export duties and to introduce more favorable taxation planning. The internationalization strategies of resource-based companies, especially the state-owned ones such as Gazprom and Rosneft, are influenced by the course of the Russian foreign policy, too.

Besides natural resource-based firms, the list of top 15 Russian investors includes only three automotive producers, two ICT companies and an insurance company. The expansion of non-natural resource-based companies abroad is a very recent phenomenon. For example, the Russian producer of anti-virus software, Kaspersky Lab as an outward investor is a lonely competitor of the outward software powerhouse of India.

Measuring outward FDI through oligarchy helps overcome that weakness of the standard trade and investment theories. It is assumed that, in order for outward FDI to take place, sufficient financial resources (wealth) are to be concentrated in the hand of individuals, or companies, or both. As a proxy for this wealth, the *Forbes* magazine list of the world's richest people (27 February 2003; referring to the situation of year 2002) has been used. It is quite notable that, of the 476 billionaires of the world in 2002, 17 came from the Russian Federation, and none from any of the other CEE countries. With this representation, the Russian Federation is the fourth billionaire country of the world, behind only the United States (222), Germany (43) and Japan (19), and ahead of, for example, Canada (15), the United Kingdom (14) and France (13). If the estimates are correct, billionaires control almost 15% of the GDP in the Russian Federation, compared with 7% in the United States and 8% in Germany.

A global comparison between the total worth of billionaires in 2002 and outward FDI stock in 2002 reveals a strong correlation between the two if the data for the whole capital export for the Russian Federation are used (0.867; see Table 3).

PROSPECTS

This does not mean however that outward FDI from the Russian Federation would fade away in the future but that its special features are to stay with us. For example, the high concentration of the outward FDI of

TABLE 3. Worth of Billionaires and Outward FDI in Selected Countries, 2002 (USD Billion)

Economy	Total worth of billionaires	Outward FDI stock
United States	703.4	1,840.0
United Kingdom	29.8	921.4
Germany	140.5	619.9
France	45.2	586.1
Netherlands	7.2	348.3
Hong Kong (China)	33.2	309.4
Japan	48.9	304.2
Switzerland/Liechtenstein	25.1	295.4
Canada	44.9	272.3
Spain	19.3	225.2
Belgium	1.0	201.5
Italy	29.6	194.5
Russian Federation	***36.6***	***155.9***
Sweden	43.9	144.4
Australia	5.4	89.7
Singapore	8.9	85.4
Denmark	5.3	75.9
Taiwan Pr. China	10.4	59.6
Brazil	8.5	54.4
Austria	1.0	42.5
Norway	1.0	38.5
Portugal	1.4	31.9
Ireland	3.3	31.6
Korea, Republic	5.0	31.1
Malaysia	8.4	28.3
South Africa	4.2	23.5
Argentina	1.6	20.5
Mexico	24.0	12.4
Chile	4.4	12.4
Israel	5.0	10.6
Greece	3.3	9.0
Venezuela	8.3	6.8
Turkey	8.9	5.0
India	17.4	4.0
Colombia	1.0	3.6
United Arab Emirates	2.0	3.1
Thailand	2.4	2.7
Indonesia	1.4	2.6
Saudi Arabia	40.2	2.1
Kuwait	5.1	1.6
Philippines	3.1	0.8
Lebanon	3.8	0.4
Rest of the world	-	209.1
Total	1,403.3	7,317.8

Source: *Forbes* magazine list of the world's richest people (27 February 2003; *http://www.forbes.com/2003/02/26/billionaireland.html*; for data on billionaires) and UNCTAD FDI/TNC database (for other data).

the Russian Federation in natural resources is expected to stay with us. It is a main difference with outward FDI from other emerging markets, which is more of a knowledge-seeking type when going abroad. It is interesting to note that even in the case of Brazil, a country which similar to the Russian Federation, suffers from the problem of round tripping (UNCTAD, 2004b), the number of TNCs investing abroad exceeded 1000 by the end of the 1990s, reflecting not just a more diversified company base for outward FDI, but also more knowledge-seeking motives. In the case of China, another emerging outward investing country, the acquisition of strategic assets (including technology and brand names) is just as important as the access to natural resources and markets (UNCTAD, 2003).

Indeed, it has been argued that knowledge should be a prime motive for Chinese firms to invest abroad, given the major cost disadvantages they have to overcome in that process (production is much cheaper in the home base). In the case of India, especially in the information technology and pharmaceutical industries, national firms have gained international competitiveness as a main source of fast expansion abroad (UNCTAD, 2004a).

Compared to those other emerging countries, Russian firms are expected to remain focused on controlling the upstream (exploration and extraction) and downstream (distribution) parts of their value chain, will also prevail, even if control of the firms proper may change hands. An additional question that may arise in the aftermath of current political changes (the conflict between the State and Yukos) is how these motivations may change if the influence of the State increases–directly or indirectly–over a range of outward investing TNCs. To what degree will that change be reflected in the priorities of those companies? Is there any reason for worry in this sense in target countries?

The most probable scenario for the future is that Russian TNCs will only marginally modify their expansion abroad (see Aton Capital, 2004, for more details). Reflecting the priorities of the government, they may somewhat slow down their expansion in other countries. They may also end up reflecting more foreign policy considerations than before. In the latter issue, however, one has to differentiate between firms that are by and large controlled by the government (e.g., Gazprom/Rosneft) and the ones over which its influence is more indirect. By all means, now that it has acquired the key oil extraction assets of Yukos, Gazprom will increasingly become the leading outward investing state-controlled oil and gas conglomerate. In turn, Lukoil will very probably remain the most important 'independent' TNC.

In both segments, the expectation is that in the future, the behavior of Russian firms will more and more approach the behavior of other global firms, located in developed countries. An indirect proof of that trend is the increasing cooperation of Russian firms with Western counterparts, both in alliances, such as the cooperation of Gazprom with Germany's E.ON, and in equity forms such as the entry of foreign investors as minority shareholders in selected Russian companies (see Table 4).

TABLE 4. Main Findings of the Research

1	The FDI outflows of the Russian Federation have always exceeded the inflows.
2	In the 1990s, official balance of payments balance of payments statistics underestimated the real volume of outward FDI.
3	In the 1990s, most of the outward FDI took forms close to 'capital flight'.
4	On the list of largest source countries of outward FDI worldwide, the Russian Federation is the only lower-middle income country; the others are all high-income countries.
5	The lower-middle-income peers of the Russian Federation, such as Turkey, South Africa, China and Brazil are at this stage net capital importing countries (their inward FDI exceeds their outward FDI).
6	The anomaly described in this article, which could be called the 'Russian paradox', is a major challenge to the standard classical theories of international trade and investment, such as the Heckscher-Ohlin-Samuelson theorem or the investment-development path.
7	Part of the capital exporting behavior of Russian firms is due to 'classical', well-documented factors such as the difficulties of the economic and business environment.
8	As a new factor, this article highlights that the existence of an 'oligarchy', which controls the natural resources of the country, as a major explanatory factor of capital exports.
9	The desire to control the full value chain of natural resources, both upstream and downstream, is an additional motivation for outward FDI, and it will remain so even after the political changes of our days.
10	This article notes the surprising absence/weakness of technology-related firms among the largest outward investing TNCs of the Russian Federation.
11	This article foresees a somewhat more active involvement of the Russian State in outward FDI through the control of some large firms such as Gazprom.

AUTHOR NOTE

Kálmán Kalotay has worked in the team preparing the *World Investment Reports* since 1996. He was also editor of the Transnational Corporations journal (1996-2004). He holds a PhD in Economics from the Corvinus University of Budapest, Hungary. He specializes on the analysis of foreign direct investment issues, especially in Central and Eastern Europe.

NOTE

1. Indonesia is so because of its strong negative FDI inflows during the crisis of the 1990s, and not so because of any major outward FDI flows.

REFERENCES

Aton Capital (2004): Russian Market 2005, 4 November, Aton Capital Group, Moscow.
Bulatov, A. (1998): Russian Direct Investment Abroad: Main Motivations in the Post-Soviet Period, Transnational Corporations, Vol. 7, No 1, pp. 69-82.
Claessens, S. and Naude, D. (1993): Recent estimates of capital flight, Working Papers of the International Economics Department of the World Bank, World Bank, Washington, D.C.
Dunning, J.H. (1981): Explaining the international direct investment position of countries: towards a dynamic or developmental approach, Weltwirtschaftliches Archiv, Vol. 119, No. 1, pp. 30-64.
Dunning, J.H. (1986): The Investment Development Cycle revisited, Weltwirtschaftliches Archiv, Vol. 122, No 4, pp. 667-677.
Heckscher, E. F. (1919): Utrikeshandelns verkan på inkomstfördelningen, Ekonomisk Tidskrift, Vol. 21, pp. 497-512; English translation: The Effect of Foreign Trade on the Distribution of Income, In: Readings in the Theory of International Trade, Ed. by Ellis, H. S., Metzler L. A., Blakiston, Garden City, NY, pp. 272-300; reprinted in: Heckscher-Ohlin Trade Theory, Ed. by Flam, H., Flanders M. J., MIT Press, Cambridge, Massachusetts, 1991.
Leontief, W. (1954): Domestic Production and Foreign Trade: The American Capital Position Reexamined, Economia Internatiozionale, Vol. 7, No 2 (February), pp. 3-32.
Ohlin, B. (1933): Interregional and International Trade, Harvard University Press, Cambridge, Massachusetts.
Ostrovsky, A. (2004): TNK-BP faces Dollars 87m back-tax bill. Financial Times, 12 November, p. 16.
Samuelson, P. (1948): International Trade and the Equalisation of Factor Prices, The Economic Journal, Vol. 58 (June), pp. 163-184.
Samuelson, P. (1949): International Factor-Price Equalisation Once Again, The Economic Journal, Vol. 58 (June), pp. 181 197.
UNCTAD (2002): World Investment Report 2002: Transnational Corporations and Export Competitiveness, United Nations, New York and Geneva.

UNCTAD (2003): China: An emerging FDI outward investor. United Nations, Geneva, *http://www.unctad.org/sections/dite_fdistat/docs/china_ebrief_en.pdf*
UNCTAD (2004a): India's outward FDI: A giant awakening? United Nations, Geneva, *http://www.unctad.org/sections/dite_dir/docs//diteiiab20041_en.pdf.*
UNCTAD (2004b): Outward FDI from Brazil: Poised to take off? United Nations, Geneva, *http://www.unctad.org/en/docs/iteiia200416_en.pdf.*

An Overview of Russia's Largest Corporations Abroad

Peeter Vahtra
Kari Liuhto

SUMMARY. Russian outward foreign direct investments have grown rapidly during the past few years. The natural-resource based companies have been the main drivers of the international growth of the Russian economy. Whereas the leading companies in oil, gas, and metal industries already rank among the top global players, the manufacturing and telecommunication industries are increasingly catching up and seeking for growth outside the Russian borders. The current article seeks to provide an overview of the international activities of the leading Russian companies in several industrial sectors with additional policy conclusions regarding the internationalisation patterns of Russian enterprises.

KEYWORDS. Russia's largest corporations, expansion abroad

Peeter Vahtra is Research Fellow and Kari Liuhto is Professor and Director, both at the Pan-European Institute, Turku School of Economics and Business Administration, Finland.

[Haworth co-indexing entry note]: "An Overview of Russia's Largest Corporations Abroad." Vahtra, Peeter, and Kari Liuhto. Co-published simultaneously in *Journal of East-West Business* (The Haworth Press, Inc.) Vol. 11, No. 3/4, 2005, pp. 23-40; and: *Expansion or Exodus: Why Do Russian Corporations Invest Abroad?* (ed: Kari Liuhto) The Haworth Press, Inc., 2005, pp. 23-40. Single or multiple copies of this article are available for a fee from The Haworth Document Delivery Service [1-800-HAWORTH, 9:00 a.m. - 5:00 p.m. (EST). E-mail address: docdelivery@haworthpress.com].

Available online at http://www.haworthpress.com/web/JEB

doi:10.1300/J097v11n03_03

INTRODUCTION

The past few years have witnessed a strong internationalisation of the Russian business. The most efficient way to bring Russia closer to the world economy is to support this integration of Russian firms into the global business. The trade rapprochement–for instance via Russia's WTO membership–is an utmost necessity but not a sufficient condition in this process, and hence more emphasis should be placed on the investment integration. Here, increasing emphasis should be given to outward investment activities of Russian corporations, whose expansion outside their domestic market is perhaps the fastest means to improve the international competitiveness of the Russian economy.

The number of academic researches on the Russian business expansion abroad remains modest despite the increasing international attention to the phenomenon. Earlier studies related to the internationalisation strategies of the Russian companies stress the limited applicability of the internationalisation theories produced in the developed West to the understanding on the foreign expansion of the Russian companies (e.g., Bulatov 1996; Efimova et al. 1996; Pchountelev 2000; Heinrich 2001).

Earlier researches also describe the activities of the Russian corporations in some individual countries, such as in Cyprus (Pelto et al. 2003), Finland (Jumpponen 2001; Vahtra & Lorentz 2004), Lithuania (Zashev 2004), and Poland (Liuhto 2002). Even a larger number of the studies deals with individual companies (e.g., Heinrich 2001; Kobyzev 2001; Liuhto 2001a/b; Peregudov 2001; Rybakov & Kapustin 2001; Survillo & Sutyrin 2001; Trofimenko 2001).

In addition, scholars have investigated reasons why the Russian companies go abroad. Economic motives have been found insufficient for explaining alone all the international activities of the Russian corporations. Therefore, the political dimension of the foreign operations should be taken into account, when the internationalisation of the Russian firms is discussed. The non-economic motives of the internationalisation become emphasised particularly in the strategic sectors of the economy, including the oil business, natural gas sector, and the metal and mining industry (e.g., Heinrich 2003; Liuhto & Jumpponen 2003a/b; Vahtra & Liuhto 2004). Due to the dominating role of the energy sector in the Russian economy, several academics have focused the outward expansion of companies operating in the energy sector (e.g., Väätänen & Liuhto 2000, Liuhto 2001a/b; Peregudov 2001; Trofimenko 2001; Heinrich 2003).

Since the United Nations Conference on Trade and Development (UNCTAD) provides a macroeconomic view on the Russian outward foreign direct investment (OFDI), the authors approach the phenomenon from the microeconomic perspective, i.e., the writers deal with the international operations of Russia's largest industrial corporations. The purpose of this article is to provide an overview on the most active outward expanders among the Russian corporations.

THE RUSSIAN OUTWARD INVESTMENT REVIEWED

In the beginning of 2004, Russia's OFDI stock amounted to $50-70 billion. With the aforementioned figure, Russia covers less than 1% of the world's OFDI stock. Even if Russia's share is minimal, one should keep in mind that the OFDI stock forms only a fraction of the Russian capital abroad. In order to estimate the total amount of the Russian capital outside Russia, one should not forget the capital flight from the country. According to the European Commission (2004), $245 billion is estimated to have flown from Russia during 1992-2002.

Kalotay (2003) suggests that the EU25 is the main destination for the Russian firms. The member states of the EU has attracted a half of all the Russian OFDI. Besides Germany, the eastern part of the EU is a particularly attractive investment target for the Russian firms. In absolute terms, Poland is the leading country in Central Eastern Europe (CEE) with nearly $1.3-billion investment from Russia. Correspondingly, Latvia and Lithuania are the leading countries measured in relative terms. In both the aforementioned countries, Russia accounts for 5% of the total inward FDI stock (see Table 1).

According to Kalotay (2003), the USA is the second largest destination of the Russian OFDI after the enlarged EU. The USA has attracted more Russian FDI than any other single country. The USA represents a quarter of the Russian OFDI stock.

The authors are convinced that the Russian corporations have a strong foothold in the CIS, even if the Russian FDI does not necessarily appear in the FDI statistics of the CIS countries. Besides statistical deficiencies, one reason for the absence of Russia in these statistics is the fact that Russian corporations have invested indirectly via another country. Russian corporations can sometimes be detected behind investments from the Bahamas, Panama, the Virgin Islands, or even some EU countries, in particular Cyprus. Russia's OFDI stock presented in Table 1 covers only a minority of the overall Russian capital in Cyprus, as Cyprus was, prior to her EU accession, perhaps the most significant transit point for Russian capital targeting to CEE.

TABLE 1. Russia's FDI Stock in the New EU Member States

Country	FDI stock *$ mn*	Share of country's total FDI stock %	Rank among investor countries	Russian FDI per host country's citizen, *$*
Cyprus (1.1.2003)	284.69	n.d.	n.d.	n.d.
Czech Republic (30.9.2004)	110.68	0.07	29	3
Estonia (30.9.2004)	102.95	1.40	10	56
Hungary (1.1.2003)	71.00	0.23	n.d.	8
Latvia (30.9.2004)	281.05	5.28	9	74
Lithuania (1.1.2004)	288.26	5.21	8	65
Malta (1.1.2004)	n.v.	n.v.	n.d.	n.d.
Poland (1.1.2004)	1,291.90	1.80	11	33
Slovakia (1.1.2004)[1]	n.v.	n.v.	n.d.	n.d.
Slovenia (1.1.2003)	n.v.	n.v.	n.d.	n.d.

n.v. = negligible value; n.d. = not defined due to insignificance of value
Source: Central banks, authors' calculations.
[1]The figure for Slovakia does not include Gazprom's acquisition of SPP and Yukos' acquisition of Transpetrol. Probably, the aforementioned investments have not been conducted directly but via another country.

The main targets for the Cypriot investments among the new and two future EU member states are Poland, the Czech Republic, Romania, Hungary, and Bulgaria. A significant amount of the Cypriot FDI in these countries (amounting to nearly $2.5 billion) is generally considered to be of Russian origin.

RUSSIAN BUSINESS EXPANSION ABROAD

UNCTAD (2004) provides a list of the 25 largest non-financial transnational companies based in CEE. Five Russian companies, namely Lukoil, Novoship, Norilsk Nickel, Primorsk Shipping, and Far Eastern Shipping, are on that list. In terms of foreign assets, Lukoil ranked as the largest transnational corporation based in ex-socialist countries with its foreign assets totalling to nearly $6 billion. With its $6 billion foreign investment, however, Lukoil did not qualify among the world's 100 most transnational corporations. Here one should keep in mind the company list provided by the UNCTAD is not fully comprehensive as it is based on an enterprise survey. In order to fulfil the obvious gaps of the list, the authors describe the foreign operations of the largest corporations in some of Russia's most outward-oriented industries.

Oil and Natural Gas Industries

Some of Russia's largest expanders can be found in the oil and natural gas sector. Russia's most transnational oil companies are privately-owned *Lukoil* and the state-owned *Rosneft*. Although their international activities cover practically the whole globe, the main production targets are the resource-rich Middle East and the CIS, particularly the Caspian Sea region. Another important location for the Russian oil companies is Eastern Europe, where they control several refining units and distribution outlets. In addition, Lukoil has widened the geographical scope of Russian oil companies to the USA. Despite the strong international presence of the industry's few leading actors, the majority of Russia's other oil producing firms can be regarded as regional players rather than global actors.

The events around the federation's formerly largest oil producer, Yukos, culminating in the acquisition of the company's main production unit by Rosneft, have considerably altered the structure of the Russian oil industry. The state is now in control not only of the transport outlets but also of a few of the country's most prominent production assets. Pre-crisis, Yukos was clearly the number one crude exporter in the country; with its main production asset now in hands of Rosneft, the latter will most likely emerge as the country's second-largest exporter after Lukoil, undoubtedly boosting up its revenues. In case Rosneft comes clean from the legal controversy over the acquisition, the company is likely to revive its investment plans for the next years, both home and abroad. The previous strategy of Rosneft suggests that no Lukoil-like downstream expansion will be witnessed, but instead the company would concentrate on foreign upstream activities and participating in intergovernmental agreements for development of oil infrastructure in Russia's 'near abroad'. Inevitably, the recent events in the oil industry indicate the switch from business-oriented internationalisation by Yukos towards the politically-orientated expansion of Rosneft.

From an international viewpoint, the current standing in the Russian oil sector, thus, includes the strengthening state grip over the sector, both in production and exports. Lukoil remains the leading actor with very aggressive expansion strategy, likely to include additional downstream acquisitions in Europe in the near future. In exports, Rosneft is likely to emerge as the main challenger of Lukoil during the upcoming years. The acquisition of the Russian state's remaining share in Lukoil by ConocoPhillips is likely to mark yet another course of change in the industry, with likely expansion of joint exploration projects in the North

Sea region, and thus further expansion of exports. The question of export infrastructure development in Russia, however, remains open with strong doubts over the northern pipeline project making the EU and US markets more accessible to companies. The fate of the foreign equity investments of Yukos, including downstream and retail outlets in the Baltic States, infrastructure assets in Slovakia and production agreements in the CIS region, remain increasingly unclear. Both the Latvian Government and the Slovakian Government have expressed their willingness for buyback of the assets in fear of legal complications shadowing Yukos. In the current situation, the option of another Russian oil major taking over Yukos' assets abroad should not be ruled out, either. For an overview of selected Russian oil companies' activities abroad, see Box 1.

BOX 1. Selected Foreign Activities of Russian Oil Companies

Lukoil, Russia's largest oil producer, has large-scale investments in foreign oil fields, production facilities and retail outlets. Nearly a fifth of the corporation's reserves are located abroad, including the Iraqi West Qurna field, the exploration rights of which remain unresolved. With estimated reserves of 20 bn barrels, West Qurna is one of the largest production fields in the world. Lukoil's other major foreign fields are located in the Azeri and Kazakh sectors of the Caspian Sea and Egypt. Even if Lukoil has considerable stakes in oil fields abroad, foreign production accounted for less than five per cent of the group's total oil and gas condensate production in 2002.

In addition to investments in exploration and production activities abroad, Lukoil has acquired refineries in Bulgaria, Romania, and Ukraine. The company also possesses an extensive retail network of some 5,000 stations, of which around 1,000 are located in other former Soviet republics and Eastern Europe. In the end of 2003, Lukoil won a tender allowing it to acquire 80% of the Serbian Beopetrol, which operates some 200 petroleum stations and several oil storage areas in Serbia. In addition to the ex-socialist countries, Lukoil has expanded to the developed West. In 2000, along with the takeover of Getty Petroleum Marketing, Lukoil acquired some 1,300 filling stations in the USA. In 2004, Lukoil acquired additional 800 stations in the USA from ConocoPhillips for the price of $266 million.

Rosneft became the second-largest Russian oil producer by acquiring the former Yukos subsidiary, Yuganskneftegaz. Russia's largest state-owned oil company's experience on international operations dates back to the Soviet era. Rosneft participates in several foreign upstream ventures. In addition, the company is engaged in intergovernmental deals over oil infrastructure development in Russia's neighbouring regions of CIS and Afghanistan. As such, Rosneft is one of the Russian Government's corporate arms overseas. The nature of the company's projects often encompasses the goals of Russian foreign policy in its neighboring countries.

Yukos acquired the position of leading Russian oil producer in 2004. The company emerged as a notable actor in the global oil business during the early 2000s. In the beginning of 2002, the company acquired 78% of the Federovsky exploration block in Kazakhstan. In the same year, Yukos bought a 49% stake in a Slovak pipeline company, Transpetrol, for the price of over $70 million. Through Transpetrol, Yukos controls the Slovakian sector of one of Russia's main pipeline export outlets, the Druzhba pipeline. In mid-2002, the company managed to obtain a controlling stake in a Lithuanian refinery, Mazeikiu Nafta, with $160 million. The future of the company, however, appears to be increasingly troubled and the deprival of its main domestic production outlet is likely to be followed by asset losses abroad as well.

Gazprom is practically Russia's natural gas industry. It covers over 80% of Russia's gas production and a similar stake of the country's gas exports. The Russian energy reform proposals foresee an increasing role of private companies in the Russian natural gas sector and access of private producers to Gazprom's transition network, but the practical decisions have been postponed on several occasions.

Gazprom has equity investments in over 20 countries, including several EU member states. Besides the EU25, Gazprom has investments in the future members of the EU, i.e., Bulgaria, Romania and Turkey, and in CIS countries. With its foreign expansion, Gazprom supports its gas exports. Due to its outward expansion, Gazprom receives revenues directly (via sales to its foreign subsidiaries) and indirectly (via the profit distribution of its foreign subsidiaries). Gazprom's investments in the EU prove that the Russian corporations may benefit directly from the enlargement even if Russia is not a member of the EU.

On one hand, Gazprom's investments in the foreign gas companies may increase the predictability of the gas supply from Russia to the EU, which is to grow significantly in the next decade. On the other hand, Gazprom is one of the main drivers of Russia's economic and political power in the EU and the CIS. In the former Soviet republics, the company is practically a sole supplier of natural gas.

As a conclusion, a handful of major companies are responsible for the lion's share of the oil and gas industry's foreign investments. These giant corporations have a considerable presence outside Russia, and they rapidly expand the scale and the scope of their foreign activities. So far, smaller companies in the Russian oil and natural gas sector have concentrated on exporting rather than establishing units abroad. However, it is probable that the smaller units will increase their presence in Russia's close-by regions in the near future. The regional internationalisation is the only option for smaller companies if they do not decide to merge either with larger Russian corporations or foreign firms. Especially in the oil industry, the concentration tendencies are highly visible with the vertically-integrated companies constantly increasing their market shares. The natural gas sector reform is projected to give rise to new private producers but remains to be implemented.

Metal and Mining Industries

The metal and mining sector accounts for over a fifth of Russia's total exports, and is currently one of the country's fastest-expanding industries. The leading metallurgical conglomerates already classify as highly global actors.

The Russian metal companies have acquired production sites mainly in the resource-rich developing countries. The country's leading aluminium company, *Russky Aljumini (RusAl)* operates a large bauxite mining complex in Africa. In the beginning of 2005, RusAl announced a large-scale acquisition in Australia, to further secure its raw material supplies. Besides mining operations abroad, RusAl owns refineries in former socialist countries.

In addition to RusAl, the other Russian metal conglomerates are seeking foothold on several strategic markets worldwide. *Norilsk Nickel* appears on UNCTAD's list of 25 most transnational companies from former socialist countries. With its recent strategic acquisitions, the company has entered the group of 10 largest gold-producers worldwide. In the steel industry, *Severstal* has entered the strategic markets of the USA and the EU pursuing a highly aggressive expansion strategy.

Alrosa is one of the world's leading diamond mining companies, responsible for almost 25% of the world's raw diamond production. Although Alrosa's domestic units cover the majority of the corporation's diamond output, the company also mines diamonds abroad. Besides foreign production, the state-owned Alrosa has opened several representative offices and trading companies overseas (see Box 2).

Although the Russian metal and mining companies are still partially on their way to reach a place on the global market, it is likely that the Russian metal giants will increase considerably their presence on the world market already in the mid-term both via establishing marketing units and buying production outlets abroad. Foreign expansion of the Russian majors serve both European and US manufacturers, who are in strong need for Russian metallurgical resources, and the Russian companies who gain a foothold on the protected markets of EU and US through the acquisitions. In upcoming years, the development in the international steel industry will be marked by the rapidly increasing Chinese exports, affecting also the internationalisation strategies of the Russian steel producers. Thus, in the face of tougher competition, more active internationalisation strategies can further be expected from the Russian steel majors.

Non-Natural Resource-Based Industries

In addition to the dominating natural resource-based sector, the companies in manufacturing industries have started their internationalisa-

BOX 2. Foreign Investments of the Largest Russian Metal and Mining Conglomerates

Russky Aljumini (RusAl) is the second largest aluminium company in the world after the US Alcoa. RusAl produces a tenth of the world's aluminium and three-quarters of Russia's output. The company exports to over 30 countries. RusAl's foreign sales account for 80% of its turnover. Europe is the largest external market, representing almost 60% of the company's export revenues. Asia accounts for over 30% and the USA practically the remaining 10%. In order to facilitate its exports, RusAl has founded representative offices at least in four countries: China, Germany, the UK, and the USA. The corporation's bauxite deficit inside Russia has pushed the company to start production abroad. In Guinea, the company manages a bauxite mining complex, Compagnie des Bauxites de Kindia. According to non-confirmed information, RusAl's investments in Guinea total $2 billion. In March 2005, RusAl announced the purchase of a 20% stake in the world's largest aluminia refinery and a major raw material provider, Queensland Aluminia Ltd. of Australia. Besides mining, RusAl owns the Oradea aluminium refinery in Romania and the Nikolayev aluminium refinery in Ukraine. The company also holds a 74% stake in the Armenal foil mill in Armenia. Reportedly, RusAl is further planning to establish a factory in India, considering spending up to $1 billion on the project in what would be one of the largest Russian investments abroad.

Norilsk Nickel is the world's largest producer of several strategic metals. Its market share is around 60% of palladium, 20% of platinum and nickel, 10% of cobalt, and 3% of copper production worldwide. The acquisition of a 20% stake in the South African gold mining company, Gold Fields Ltd. in early 2004, strengthened Norilsk Nickel's position as one of the leading gold producers worldwide. To date, the deal is the single largest foreign investment made by a Russian company. In order to support its foreign sales, the company has acquired a London-based metal trading company, Norimet Ltd. In 2003, Norilsk Nickel bought a 51% stake in a US company, Stillwater Mining, in a $257-million deal. Stillwater Mining is the sole producer of platinum-group metals in the USA and the fifth largest producer in the world.

Severstal ranks among the world's top 20 steel companies. The company's exports are targeted to over 100 destinations worldwide. The company is one of the most aggressive Russian industrial expanders abroad. In the end of 2003, Severstal won the auction to buy Rouge Industries, the fifth largest steel producer in the USA. The acquisition would provide a means to circumvent the US steel import restrictions and increase Severstal's global recognition. For managing its US assets, Severstal has established an affiliate, Severstal North America Inc, in the country. Apart from its acquisition in the USA, Severstal is eyeing a giant target in the CIS, Ukraine's largest steel producer, Kryvorizhstal, participating in the revised privatisation process. In the beginning of 2005, Severstal reached an agreement to buy a 62% stake in an Italian steel product manufacturer, Lucchini SpA, for an estimated price of $430 million. Immediately after the Italian acquisition, Severstal announced its bid for a Canadian steel company, Stelco, on the verge of bankruptcy. The Russian major has been reported to eye additional assets in the US and Czech Republic. Severstal has also established a joint venture with a European group, Arcelor, for the manufacturing of hot galvanised rolled products for the European market. Severstal holds 75% of the shares in this venture.

tion. Although only one non-natural resource-based company, namely *OMZ*, can be placed among the most transnational industrial corporations in Russia, several manufacturing companies have established production and marketing units abroad.

OMZ (Uralmash-Izhora Group) is the largest heavy engineering corporation in Russia. The company controls 70% of the Russian market for oil and gas drilling equipment, 60% of the special steels market, 80% of the metallurgical equipment market, 50% of the nuclear power plant equipment market, and more than 90% of the mining equipment market. OMZ's products are exported to over 30 countries. Altogether Asia accounts for 60%, the CIS 21%, and Europe 19% of the consortium's exports. The company possesses production, marketing, and investment units overseas. Box 3 outlines the main foreign subsidiaries of OMZ.

AvtoVaz is Russia's largest automobile producer and ranks among the country's 10 biggest corporations in terms of sales. As the Russian car producers suffer from weaker output quality compared to their foreign rivals, the company's main competitive advantage can be found in the low-priced automobile segment. The most potential foreign target markets for AvtoVaz, hence, include the CIS and the developing countries (see Box 4).

The company's exports have grown slightly during the past few years. Besides the exports to some 40 countries, the company has established considerable foreign presence during the past few years, operating several production and distribution subsidiaries overseas. The decreasing domestic demand has pushed Russian car producers to seek growth from other developing markets of the world. The locations of

BOX 3. Foreign Investments of OMZ

COUNTRY	COMPANY	ACTIVITIES	OMZ'S STAKE %
Armenia	OOO OMZAR	Investing activities	100
Br. Virgin Islands	UHM Investments Ltd.	Investing activities	100
	Shipley Trading Ltd. BVI	Investing activities	100
Czech Republic	Skoda Steel	Castings production	100
	Skoda JS	Nuclear equipment production	100
Netherlands	Friede Goldman Marketing	Sales of engineering services	75
	United Heavy B.V.	Investing activities	100
	UHM Investments NV	Investing activities	100
Romania	UPET S.A.	Production of metal valves, mobile rings and offshore rigs' components	66
Tunis	UHM Tunissia	Representative office	95
Ukraine	OAO CBK Korall	Design and R&D for shipbuilding industry and drilling platforms	30
USA	BioLink Technologies Inc.	Development, manufacturing and marketing of fingerprint biometric products	39
	FGL Buyer LLC	Naval architecture and marine engineering in offshore drilling	75
	OMZ Investments Co.	Investing activities	100
	Friede Goldman United Ltd.	Royalties and license fees from FGL Buyer LLC	75

BOX 4. Main Overseas Units of AvtoVaz

COUNTRY/COMPANY	ACTIVITIES	SHARE, %
Cyprus		
Lada International Ltd.	Car distribution	100
Egypt		
Lada-Egypt	Car assembly plant	n.d.
Finland		
Oy Konela Ab	Car distribution	70
Germany		
FerroVAZ GmbH	Metal production	50
Greece		
Lada Hellas S.A.	Car distribution	50
Lada Parts Hellas S.A.	Spare parts distribution	50

AvtoVaz' foreign units range from neighboring Finland to the African continent.

Another example on a foreign-oriented, non-natural resource-based company can be found in the foodstuffs industry. *Wimm-Bill-Dann* (WBD) is the market leader in Russia in a wide range of juices, yoghurt, and baby food products. Even if Wimm-Bill-Dann is primarily focusing on the domestic market, it additionally has a strong position in the CIS region. The company also sells its products to Canada, Germany, Israel, the Netherlands, the UK and the USA through both its own distribution network and independent distributors. Recently, the company has entered the Baltic markets, on which it looks for a substantial market share (see Box 5).

Wimm-Bill-Dann has production units in Kyrgyzstan and Ukraine. In 2000, the company acquired an 84% stake in a Kyrgyz dairy plant, Bishkeksut, for a modest $450,000. A year later, WBD acquired a 60% stake in a Ukrainian plant, Kiev Dairy No 3, in a $4-million deal. In 2002, WBD strengthened its presence in Ukraine by acquiring an 82% stake in the Ukrainian Kharkovsky dairy plant for $5 million, followed by the acquisition of a 76% stake in the Burynsky Dairy Powder Factory for $2 million.

Despite WBD's foreign production facilities, the bulk of the company's production is carried out inside Russia. Since the company's business is continuously growing, its future acquisitions may, however, include the companies from CEE. It is likely that the CIS will, neverthe-

BOX 5. Foreign Units of Wimm-Bill-Dann

COUNTRY	COMPANY	ACTIVITIES	WBD'S SHARE, %
Canada, Germany, Israel, Netherlands, UK, USA	Distribution centres	Sales, marketing	100
Kyrgyzstan	Bishkeksut	Dairy plant	84
Ukraine	Kiev Dairy	Dairy plant	58
	Kharovsky	Dairy plant	82
	Burynsky	Dairy powder factory	76

less, hold the largest potential for WBD's foreign operations in the short term.

The third example of the outward-oriented non-natural resource-based industry is mobile telecommunication, currently one of the fastest-growing Russian industries. The number of mobile phone users has more than doubled during the past year, and the current amount of some 60 million mobile customers is not even near the market saturation. The three dominant companies in the mobile communication market, *MTS, VimpelCom*, and *MegaFon*, account for close to 90% of the market.

MTS' market share in Russia was around 40% in 2003. Besides its leading position in the Russian markets, MTS has expanded its activities abroad. In 2003, MTS acquired the controlling stake in the largest mobile operator in Ukraine, UMC. The price of the purchase was $194 million. In 2003, MTS further invested over $60 million in Ukraine. In Belarus, MTS holds a 49% stake in Mobile TeleSystems LLC. In addition to its operations on the Ukrainian and Belarus markets, MTS is reported to have interest in other CIS countries and Bulgaria.

Also the other two major players in Russian telecommunication markets have penetrated the lucrative CIS markets. Outside Russia, *VimpelCom* currently operates in Kazakhstan. *MegaFon* entered the Tajikistan markets already in the early 2000s. All three companies reportedly eye additional assets in the CIS countries, which hold incomparable market potential for Russian operations due to their low penetration and competition levels.

UNCTAD indicates that Lukoil, along with Norilsk Nickel and three Russian shipping companies, ranks among the 10 most transnational companies based in the ex-CMEA. The authors consider that the shipping companies should be excluded from the list since the outward expansion of these companies reminds one more of a technical exercise rather than genuine internationalisation, because the foreign-flagging ships do not mean that the firm would have become more committed to foreign operations or that the business practices would have changed. Sea transportation is an international business by definition, and hence those shipping companies dealing with international trade do not become global as such, but rather they are born global.

The researchers believe that Russia's ten largest industrial companies having established the strongest international presence are Gazprom, Lukoil, Russky Aljumini, Norilsk Nickel, Severstal, Itera, Yukos, OMZ, Rosneft and Alrosa.

The Russian metal conglomerates are currently pursuing the most active internationalisation strategies and both Norilsk Nickel and Severstal are likely to increase their foreign presence considerably during the upcoming years. The internationalisation of the Russian oil sector largely lies on the shoulders of Lukoil, who recently announced plans to enter the Finnish market by acquiring the number two petroleum retailer in the country. Further downstream acquisitions in the EU countries and in the USA are also likely to be witnessed in the near future. The heavy engineering sector currently does not hold strong potential for expansion outside the CIS, but the former Soviet republics are likely to provide the most lucrative markets for the companies in the sector in the near term. The CIS markets hold additional potential for the Russian telecommunications sector with all three leading Russian players–MTS, VimpelCom, and Megafon–having expanded their operations to the region. In other manufacturing industries, Wimm-Bill-Dann is actively expanding out of the Russian market, and is eyeing the Baltic countries in addition to its present operations in the CIS (see Table 2).

CONCLUSIONS

From the Russian perspective, the outward expansion of the Russian firms is essential for both the individual companies and the Russian economy as a whole. The companies must become more international in order to survive in the global competition, which will become fiercer even on the domestic market when Russia gains a membership in the WTO. Correspondingly, the Russian economy requires a structural reform and competitiveness improvement to transform the country from the natural-resource-based economy towards a modern service and in-

TABLE 2. Russia's 10 Most Transnational Corporations in Terms of Foreign Assets

Company	Main countries/regions abroad	Type of activity abroad	Estimated value of foreign assets
Gazprom	Several countries in the CIS, CEE and EU plus Southeast Europe	Trading, distribution, and marketing of gas, manufacturing of petrochemicals and gas, pipeline construction	Unknown but very considerable
Lukoil	Azerbaijan, (Iraq), Kazakhstan, Egypt, Columbia, Iran, Saudi-Arabia, Bulgaria, Ukraine, Romania, Baltic States, USA	Production and exploration of oil and gas, oil refining, retailing and marketing of petroleum	~ $7-9 billion
RusAl	Armenia, Romania, Ukraine, Guinea, Germany, USA, China, UK	Refining, processing and production of aluminium, bauxite mining, sales and marketing units overseas	~ $2-3 billion
Norilsk Nickel	UK, USA, Switzerland, Belgium, South Africa	Sales, marketing, and production of platinum-group metals, production of cobalt, mining and production of gold	~ $2 billion
Severstal	USA, Italy	Steel production	~ $1.5 billion
Itera	USA, Armenia, Belarus, Estonia, Georgia, Latvia, Moldova, Turkmenistan, Uzbekistan	Headquarters (USA), gas distribution, plastic manufacturing, fertiliser production, metal production, pipeline construction	~ $1 billion
Yukos	UK, Slovakia, Kazakhstan, Lithuania, Austria, China	Oil exploration, process technology, pipeline construction, oil transportation, oil refining	~ $1 billion
OMZ	Romania, Netherlands, USA, Armenia, British Virgin Islands, Tunisia, Ukraine	Production of metal devices, investing and sales activities, technology development, engineering services	...
Rosneft	Kazakhstan, Algeria, Columbia, Afghanistan	Oil and gas production, field development, reconstruction of oil and gas infrastructure	~ $0.5 billion
Alrosa	Angola, Belgium, Israel, UK	Diamond mining, sales and marketing, product development	~ $0.5 billion

novation-oriented society. The outward expansion is perhaps the most efficient way to force companies to change their old patterns.

The Russian Government's policy towards the Russian companies' internationalisation is currently not supportive enough. The government should encourage firms particularly in non-natural resource-based industries to expand their operations particularly in the developed West, since the expansion towards the developing countries and the CIS does not force the Russian companies to transform their business practices as fast as the developed West. The encouragement could occur for instance in a form of providing risk finance, know-how and networks. In addition, the foreign expansion of the companies in natural-resource-based sectors, and energy in particular, is continuously overshadowed by Russian political interests 'near abroad'. By promoting transparent and non-politically motivated investments abroad, the Russian firms would face a completely different attitude milieu in the recipient countries. Given the deep-rooted history-based resistance towards Russia's political and economic dominance in the former socialist bloc, the ultimate goal behind the internationalisation of the Russian companies play a significant role in how these companies are perceived in the host countries.

From the host countries' point of view, the Russian firms conducting legal and non-politically-motivated business are the most welcomed. The host countries' attitudes towards the large natural resource-based conglomerates depend to which extent they execute Russia's foreign policy. The internationalisation of politically-tied companies such as Gazprom and RAO UES are particularly puzzling for those host countries, which struggle against the Russian dominance in their strategic industries. In several occasions, the economic resources of Russia serve to develop her political influence in the neighbouring regions with the state-run resource-based conglomerates serving as the main drivers of Russian 'soft power' in the region.

It should be remembered, though, that the Russian companies may have a Janus-face, i.e., they may simultaneously play different games in different regions. The expansion of Russian companies in the CIS may be politically shadowed, whereas elsewhere they may operate purely according to business logic. It is not completely unheard of that the same company could even have a third face, i.e., it may also be involved in non-legal activities in some developing country. Involvement in an illegal armament trade can be taken as an example of the aforementioned.

The outward expansion of Russian companies will be dominated by the strategic industries for years to come, and hence the extensive internationalisation of purely business-oriented companies could remain wishful thinking in the near future. However, in the longer run, the foreign activities of Russian companies guided by mere economic rationality are likely to expand, especially if the country succeeds in breaking its critical dependency on the exports of the strategic natural resources, and the Russian Government's policies towards the internationalisation become less politically-oriented. If this is to happen, it seems evident that the host country policies, particularly in the ex-CMEA, towards the Russian business entry will become more neutral.

In the European Union, the operations of the Russian firms in the internal market, and vice versa, the activities of the EU-based companies in Russia strengthen the linkage between the Union and Russia. Furthermore, the Russian companies' investments in the EU aid in building the Common European Economic Space between the Union and Russia, and advance the energy dialog between the parties.

REFERENCES

Aldenderfer, M.S. and R.K. Blashfield. 1984. *Cluster Analysis*. Newbury Park: Sage.

Bartlett, C.A. and S. Ghoshal. 1989. *Managing Across Borders. The Transnational Solution*. Boston: Harvard Business School Press.

Bulatov, A. 1998. Russian Direct Investment Abroad–Main Motivations in the Post-Soviet Period. *Transnational Corporations* 7: 69-82.

Carper, W.B. and W.E. Snizek. 1980. The Nature and Types of Organizational Taxonomies: An Overview. *Academy of Management Review* 5: 65-75.

Cheklina, T. 1991. Joint Ventures in Eastern Europe. *Foreign Trade* 8: 25-27.

Doty, H.D. and W.H. Glick. 1994. Typologies as a Unique Form of Theory Building: Toward Improved Understanding and Modeling. *Academy of Management Review* 19: 230-251.

Efimova, E.G., V.I. Kapustkin, and S.F. Sutyrin. 1996. Comparative analysis of foreign entry strategies of Western and the CIS firms in each others markets. *Proceedings of the University of Vaasa* 18: 166-179.

Economic Intelligence Unit. 2004. *Country Report Russia March 2004*.

European Commission. 2004. *Communication from the Commission to the Council and the European Parliament on relations with Russia*.

Expert Rating Agency. 2004. Database "EXPERT-200" [Cited 1 December 2004]. Available from World Wide Web:<http://www.raexpert.ru/ratings/exp200/index.php3?inc=6&path=3&lh=1&yearR=2003&lang=eng>

Ghoshal, S. and N. Nohria. 1993. Horses for Courses: Organizational Forms for Multinational Corporations. *Sloan Management Review* 34: 23-35.

Hamilton, G., ed. 1986. *Red Multinationals or Red Herrings?–The Activities of Enterprises from Socialist Countries in the West*. London: Pinter.

Harzing, A.W. 2000. An Empirical Analysis and Extension of the Bartlett and Ghoshal Typology of Multinational Companies. *Journal of International Business Studies* 31: 101-120.

Heinrich, A. 2001. Internationalisation, Market Structures and Enterprise Behaviour–The Janus-faced Russian Gas Monopoly Gazprom. In K. Liuhto, ed. *East Goes West–The Internationalization of Eastern Enterprises*: 51-87. Lappeenranta: Lappeenranta University of Technology.

Heinrich, A. 2003. Internationalisation of Russia's Gazprom. *Journal of East European Management Studies* 8: 46-66.

Hill, M. 1986. Soviet and Eastern European Company Activity in the United Kingdom and Ireland. In G. Hamilton, ed., *Red Multinationals or Red Herrings?–The Activities of Enterprises from Socialist Countries in the West*: 17-87. London: Pinter.

Jumpponen, J. 2001. 'Made in Russia' in Finland–Some Preliminary Findings. In Kari Liuhto, ed., *East Goes West–The Internationalization of Eastern Enterprises*: 223-232. Lappeenranta: Lappeenranta University of Technology.

Kalotay, K. 2003. Outward Foreign Direct Investment from Economies in Transition in a Global Context. *Journal of East European Management Studies* 8: pp. 6-24.

Kobyzev, S.B. 2001. Internationalization of Russian Pulp and Paper Company. In Kari Liuhto, ed., *East Goes West–The Internationalization of Eastern Enterprises*: 162-178. Lappeenranta: Lappeenranta University of Technology.

Leong, S.M. and T.T. Chin. 1993. Managing Across Borders: An Empirical Test of the Bartlett and Ghoshal (1989) Organizational Typology. *Journal of International Business Studies* 24: 449-464.

Liuhto, K. 2001a. A Russian Oil and Gas Giant Goes West. In Kari Liuhto, ed., *East Goes West–The Internationalization of Eastern Enterprises*: 1-50. Lappeenranta: Lappeenranta University of Technology.

Liuhto, K. 2001b. Russian Gas and Oil Giant Conquer Markets in the West: Evidence on the Internationalization of Gazprom and LUKoil. *Journal of East-West Business* 7: 31-72.

Liuhto, K. 2002. Russian Direct Investments in Poland. In Kari Liuhto, ed., *Business in Poland*: 368-379. Lappeenranta: Lappeenranta University of Technology.

Liuhto, K. and J. Jumpponen. 2001. International Activities of Russian Corporations–Where Does Russian Business Expansion Lead? *Russian Economic Trends* 10: 19-29.

Liuhto, K. and J. Jumpponen. 2003a. *Russian Eagle Has Landed Abroad. Evidence Concerning the Foreign Operations of Russia's 100 Biggest Exporters and Banks.* Lappeenranta: Lappeenranta University of Technology.

Liuhto, K. and J. Jumpponen. 2003b. Russian Corporations and Banks Abroad. *Journal of East European Management Studies*. 8: 25-44.

Matejka, H. 1988. More Joint Enterprises within CMEA. In J. Hardt and C.H. Macmillan, eds., *Planned Economies–Confronting the Challenges of the 1980s*: 171-189. Cambridge: Cambridge University Press.

McMillan, C. H. 1987. *Multinationals from the Second World–Growth of Foreign Investment by Soviet and East European State Enterprises*. London: MacMillan Press.

Pchounetlev, V. (2000). *Internationalisation Strategies of Russian Companies*, Paper presented at the Second International Conference 'Transition and Enterprise Restructuring in Eastern Europe,' 17-19 August 2000, Hellerod, Denmark.

Pelto, E., P. Vahtra, and K. Liuhto. 2003. *Cyp-Rus Investment Flows to Central and Eastern Europe* [online]. Pan-European Institute, Turku School of Economics [cited 1 February 2005]. Available from World Wide Web: <http://www.tukkk.fi/pei/pub>

Peregudov, S.P. 2001. Large Corporations as National and Global Players: The Case of Lukoil. In K. Segbers, ed., *Explaining Post-Soviet Patchworks: Actors and sectors in Russia between accommodation and resistance to globalization*: 116-135.

Porter, M.E. 1980. *Competitive Strategy: Techniques for Analyzing Industries and Competitors*. New York: Free Press.

Porter, M.E. 1985 *Competitive Advantage: Creating and Sustaining Superior Performance*. New York: Free Press.

Rich, P. 1992. The Organizational Taxonomy: Definition and Design. *Academy of Management Review* 17: 758-781.

Standard & Poor's. 2004. *Russian Transparency and Disclosure Survey 2004.*

Rybakov, F.F. and E.D. Kapustin. 2001. One Sky for Everybody? In K. Liuhto, ed., *East Goes West–The Internationalization of Eastern Enterprises*: 178-207. Lappeenranta: Lappeenranta University of Technology.

Sokolov, S. 1991a. Companies Set Up Abroad with Soviet Capital. *Foreign Trade* 10: 15-17.

Sokolov, S. 1991b. Sovetskiy kapital za rubezhom. *Ekonomika i Zhizn* 14: 1-15.

Survillo, V.G. and S.F. Sutyrin. 2001. The Way of Sibirsky Aluminium. In K. Liuhto, ed., *East Goes West–The Internationalization of Eastern Enterprises*: 134-161. Lappeenranta: Lappeenranta University of Technology.

Tikhomirov, V. 1997. Capital Flight from Post-Soviet Russia. *Europe-Asia Studies* 49: 591-615.

Trofimenko, O. 2001. In Search of the New Lights–Internationalization of RAO UES. In K. Liuhto, ed., *East Goes West–The Internationalization of Eastern Enterprises*: 113-133. Lappeenranta: Lappeenranta University of Technology.

UNCTAD. 2004. *World Investment Report 2004: The Shift Towards Services.* New York and Geneva: United Nations.

Vahtra, P. and K. Liuhto. 2004. *Expansion or Exodus?–Foreign Operations of Russia's Largest Corporations* [online]. Pan-European Institute, Turku School of Economics [cited 1 February 2005]. Available from World Wide Web: <http://www.tukkk.fi/pei/pub>

Vahtra, P. and H. Lorentz. 2004. *Russian Involvement in Finnish Companies-Energy Sector in Focus* [online]. Pan-European Institute, Turku School of Economics [cited 1 February 2005]. Available from World Wide Web: <http://www.tukkk.fi/pei/pub>

Väätänen, J. and K. Liuhto. 2000. East Goes West–The Internationalization of Russian Corporations. *Proceedings of 9th IMDA Conference.* San Jose.

World Bank. 2004. *From Transition to Development: A Country Economic Memorandum for the Russian Federation* [online]. [cited 1 February 2005] Available from World Wide Web: <http://www.worldbank.org.ru>

Zaleski, E. 1986. Socialist multinationals in developing countries. In G. Hamilton, ed., *Red Multinationals or Red Herrings?–The Activities of Enterprises from Socialist Countries in the West*: 156-184. London: Pinter.

Zashev, P. 2004. *Russian Investments in Lithuania–Politics, Business, Corporate Culture.* Pan-European Institute [online]. Pan-European Institute, Turku School of Economics [cited 1 February 2005]. Available from World Wide Web: <http://www.tukkk.fi/pei/pub>

Russian Companies in Old EU Member States: The Case of Germany

Andreas Heinrich

SUMMARY. In Germany small businesses seem to dominate Russian investment activities in number. Larger, export-oriented Russian companies, mostly from the raw materials sector, use Germany as an entry to Europe–primarily to the old EU member states–utilizing its technological and intellectual infrastructure. However, the majority of investment activities are unspecific and insignificant. Driven by market seeking motives, the Russian companies have established primarily representative offices and marketing subsidiaries. The only remarkable exception is Gazprom, which is involved in more specific and significant investments in Germany. *[Article copies available for a fee from The Haworth Document Delivery Service: 1-800-HAWORTH. E-mail address: <docdelivery@haworthpress.com> Website: <http://www.HaworthPress.com> © 2005 by The Haworth Press, Inc. All rights reserved.]*

KEYWORDS. Russian firms in Germany

Andreas Heinrich is Research Associate, Institute for World Economics and International Management (IWIM), University of Bremen, Germany.

The author would like to thank Hilary Abuhove, Tanja Galander and Heiko Pleines for their useful information, comments and support.

[Haworth co-indexing entry note]: "Russian Companies in Old EU Member States: The Case of Germany." Heinrich, Andreas. Co-published simultaneously in *Journal of East-West Business* (The Haworth Press, Inc.) Vol. 11, No. 3/4, 2005, pp. 41-59; and: *Expansion or Exodus: Why Do Russian Corporations Invest Abroad?* (ed: Kari Liuhto) The Haworth Press, Inc., 2005, pp. 41-59. Single or multiple copies of this article are available for a fee from The Haworth Document Delivery Service [1-800-HAWORTH, 9:00 a.m. - 5:00 p.m. (EST). E-mail address: docdelivery@haworthpress.com].

Available online at http://www.haworthpress.com/web/JEB

doi:10.1300/J097v11n03_04

INTRODUCTION

One of the first casualties of the dissolution of the Soviet Union was its centrally planned economic system, which had effectively isolated the country from global markets. The Russian Federation has been increasingly exposed to global influences ever since, forcing it towards greater integration into global markets. One important phenomenon of this greater integration has been the internationalization of the Russian companies.

Internationalization means the development of cross-border activities between and within companies by expanding sales markets and investing in international activities over an extended period of time. These activities are traditionally measured by exports and outward foreign direct investment.[1]

This article deals with Germany as the destination for the internationalization of companies from Russia. Germany was chosen as an example for old EU member states because of its enormous importance for Russia as a trading partner, regarding both imports and exports, as well as a major destination of Russian outward FDI. This research analyzes the different motives for internationalization of Russian companies active in Germany.

After the theoretical grounding of the motives of internationalization, a general overview of Russia's internationalization is presented describing the trade and investment flows from Russia to Germany. The structure of the Russian internationalization in Germany and the motives to invest in Germany as an old EU member country will thereby be elaborated upon. The paper is enriched by examples of Russian companies doing business in Germany.

This case study selected the basic indicators of internationalization–sales and outward FDI–and, additionally, strategic partnerships as a means of market entry to analyze the motives for these internationalizations.

THE MOTIVES FOR INTERNATIONALIZATION

The internationalization of a firm is reflected in its process of international market expansion and investment over time which can be measured in its international sales and outward FDI. Internationalization refers to the way a company strategically exploits location advantages and economies of scale to leverage a competitive edge world-wide. The concept of internationalization describes the establishment of a network of cross-border activities between and within companies in which any or all of the company's departments may be involved. Three main approaches to research internationalization have emerged in the literature: FDI theory (including transaction cost analysis), stage models, and network perspectives. However, only the FDI theory makes distinctive assumptions about the motivation of FDI, and therefore this paper focuses on this theoretical approach.

The general body of FDI theory has emerged from various theoretical contributions. A common feature of the FDI theory is that foreign direct investment is the response by a firm to a particular type of market failure. The basic idea is that incomplete contracts and missing markets give rise to the possibility of opportunistic behavior in serving a foreign market at a distance (Williamson 1975) and for this reason a firm prefers to replace external contracts with direct ownership and internal hierarchies. The original FDI theory (Hymer 1976) starts from the principle that multinational enterprises operate at an inherent disadvantage with respect to national firms because of the additional costs of doing business abroad. These costs derive from communications and management problems, consumer attitudes to foreign firms, language, culture and other operational barriers, and the costs of being outside the normal business and government networks. Thus, a commitment in a foreign market has to possess compensating advantages such as superior technology or products, or firm-level economies of scale.

Dunning (1980, 1988) suggests that for a firm to undertake FDI, ownership-specific advantages must be obtained. The eclectic paradigm claims that foreign direct investment arises when three conditions are satisfied (the so-called OLI paradigm: ownership, location, internalization). First, the firm must possess specific ownership advantages (tangible or intangible) not available to other firms, such as a superior technology, patents on particular products, a brand name, a trademark or other indication of product quality. Second, the foreign market should offer some location advantages–specific in their origin to particular locations and which can only be utilized on-site, like natural resources, most kinds of labor, proximity to markets, but also the legal and commercial environment in which the assets are used (market structures, legislation, etc.)–that make it more profitable to serve the foreign market by local production rather than by exporting or importing (e.g., high tariff barriers to exports or anti-dumping regulations). Third, there should be an internalization advantage in that the firm believes that its ownership advantages are best exploited internally. This advantage derives from the difficulties that arise in writing enforceable and controllable contracts with potential foreign partners (market failures) that generate an income that approximates the true worth of the advantage being marketed.

There is a complex relationship between ownership and location specific advantages. While the home country normally gives rise to ownership advantages, location specific advantages are derived from FDI in a host county. "*The possession of ownership advantages determines which firms will supply a particular foreign market, whereas the pattern of location endowments explains whether the firm will supply that market by exports (trade) or by local production (non-trade)*" (Dunning 1980: 11).

In summary, the main standard motives for internationalization are market seeking, resource seeking, efficiency seeking and strategic asset seeking (Buckley 1988; Dunning 1993, 1998).

1. *Market seeking:* The FDI theory suggests that involvement in foreign markets is strongly linked to the absolute size of the host market and the potential for market growth. Such market-seeking FDI is usually seen as a response to the costs of serving a foreign market at a distance. Generally speaking, the larger the foreign market the greater is the tendency of the supplying firm both to prefer foreign production and to wish to own and control that production in the form of FDI.
2. *Resource seeking:* Physical resource-seeking applies to transnational corporations seeking access to raw materials abroad, to obtain security of supply.
3. *Efficiency seeking:* Foreign operations to reduce input costs are strongly associated with manufacturing industry, e.g., lower labor costs in the foreign country.
4. *Strategic asset seeking:* 'Strategic asset or capability seeking' (Dunning 1993) describes attempts to secure the input of key elements in the production process such as technology, professional, managerial, and financial skills, knowledge of various types, and marketing expertise. One common way to acquire these assets is to form a joint venture with a partner with whom, and from whom, these capabilities can be learned.

Additionally, for companies from CEE, Kalotay (2003: 18) asserts that they are often escaping a difficult and partly unstable business environment rather than using specific ownership advantages; this mindset can be called ownership disadvantage. Therefore, a possible reaction to an unstable political and economical environment is capital flight–above all important for Russian companies in the early 1990s. This motive should be called stability seeking.

RUSSIAN INTERNATIONALIZATION TO GERMANY

Trade

Trade liberalization became the first means of re-integration of Russia into the world economy and, therefore, of internationalization. Russian foreign merchandise trade in 2003 amounted to some USD 209 bn, giving a surplus of USD 60 bn. The main reasons for this increase in trade were high prices for exports, especially the high oil price since 2000, and stable growth in final consumption and investment. According to WTO (2004: 19), Russia was responsible for 1.8% of the world's exports (rank 17) and for 1.0% of the world's imports (rank 23).

Russia's foreign merchandise trade structure is quite unbalanced. Russia is primarily an exporter of energy sources and raw materials and an importer of manufactured and half-finished products as well as consumer and capital goods. In particular, its main exports continue to be oil, oil products and natural gas, followed by metals and metal products. Its main imports are machinery, equipment, motor vehicles, foodstuffs and chemical products (German Foreign Office, February 2004). In 2001, nearly two-thirds of Russia's 15 biggest exporting companies belonged to the oil and gas industry and the rest to the metals industry. Together these 15 firms accounted for about half of all Russian exports by value.

The trade with commercial services is becoming more and more important for Russia; in 2003, Russia exported commercial services worth USD 16 bn, while it imported these services for USD 27 bn. Russia ranked in 27th place among the world's largest exporters with 0.9% of the world's total commercial service exports and in 18th place (with 1.5%) among importers (WTO 2004: 21). The exports in commercial services marked a new peak in 2003 with more growth potential in the IT sector, for instance. However, it should be noticed that the export of services has been used as a vehicle for capital flight in the past. Therefore, the validity of these figures is only of limited scope.

Throughout the 1990s, Germany was Russia's largest trading partner. In 2000, both nine per cent of Russia's exports went to Germany, while nine per cent of its imports stemmed from there (Götz/Meier 2001). In 2003, nearly eight per cent of Russia's exports went to Germany, while more than 14% of Russia's imports came from Germany (Ost-Ausschuss der deutschen Wirtschaft 2004: 9).

The development of the mutual trade was characterized by stability of exports with a slight downturn caused by the Russian financial crisis in 1998. However, in 2000 Russian exports turned up sharply, due to the extraordinary rise in price of fossil fuels and other raw materials. Imports have been more volatile and eroded after 1998. In 2002, exports decreased, while imports from Germany increased to its pre-crisis high. In 2003, exports as well as imports increased significantly and both reached a new peak in mutual trade (see Table 1).

However, an unbalanced trade structure is also typical for Russia's economic relations with Germany. Russia's exports to Germany consists predominantly of raw materials. In 2003, raw materials amounted to nearly three quarters of the German imports from Russia. The largest components were crude oil and natural gas, followed by ferrous metals, timber and lumber. Russia also exported half-finished products (18%), such as metals (copper, nickel, aluminum), pulp, and paper or petrochemicals, and fore-products (5%). The share of manufactured products amounted to a modest 3% (German Embassy Moscow 2004). In 2003, Russia exported some 30 billion cubic meters of natural gas to Germany and supplied a third of Germany's total demand (Gazprom and Ruhrgas company information). With approximately 34 million tons of crude

TABLE 1. Russia's Trade Balance with Germany (USD Billion)

	Exports	Imports	Total	Balance
1995	6.2	6.5	12.7	−0.3
1996	6.7	5.2	11.9	+1.5
1997	6.5	6.6	13.1	−0.1
1998	5.7	5.5	11.2	+0.2
1999	6.2	4.2	10.4	+2.0
2000	9.2	3.9	13.1	+5.3
2001	9.2	5.8	15.0	+3.4
2002	8.0	6.6	14.6	+1.4
2003	10.4	8.1	18.5	+2.3

Sources: Goskomstat 2003b: 636; BOFIT Weekly, No. 8, 20 February 2004.

oil, or an import share of 32%, Russia was also Germany's biggest supplier of crude oil (Bundesanstalt für Aussenhandel).

The export of services to Germany is still small, as the example of the IT sector shows. In cooperation with German businesses Russian software firms made USD 33-37 mn in revenues in 2002. The Russian IT specialists are generally cheaper than their Western colleagues. However, they are quite a bit more expensive than their Indian competitors–the benchmark in the offshore software business–and less well-known on the German market (Bruggmann 2003).

At the same time, Russian imports from Germany were strongly dominated by manufactured products, which amounted to 83% of total imports. Other important items in the Russian imports from Germany were fore-products (9%) and food (5%), followed by half-finished products (1.5%), luxury goods (1.2%) and raw materials (0.3%) (German Embassy Moscow 2004).

The unequal structure of mutual trade hampers balanced growth of bilateral trade for two reasons. Firstly, the volume of the Russian exports in value terms is substantially influenced by heavy oscillations of prices for energy sources and raw materials. Secondly, the demand for the Russian exports relative to Germany's gross national product is diminishing. Consequently Russia's earnings from foreign trade and import potential are subject to fluctuations and uncertainty (Götz/Meier 2001).

FDI

Volume

The outward investments of Russian companies have grown significantly since 1997. Russia's outward FDI flow tripled to USD 3.2 bn, while the outward FDI stock nearly doubled to USD 6.4 bn. The FDI stock skyrocketed again in 2001, when it more than doubled to USD 20.1 bn followed by steady strong growth in the following years.

Russia, with an outward FDI stock of USD 52 bn in 2003, comprises the largest share of outward FDI from CEE countries. Nevertheless, Russia's outward FDI stock amounted to just a mere 0.6% of the world's FDI stock. However, the outward FDI stock represents only a fraction of the total Russian capital abroad; capital flight is not included (UNCTAD 2004a: 72; Vahtra/Liuhto 2004: 9).

A substantial part of Russia's outward investment goes in the margins of capital flight as one side effect of economic liberalization. During the 1990s, the internationalization of Russian companies and the growth of Russian migrant communities in many Western countries have created a large variety of geographic locations of Russian flight capital. In more general terms, the major part of Russian capital is transferred to (1) Western countries which have established and stable banking systems; (2) countries with large local Russian-speaking communities; (3) countries that have liberal offshore legislation; and (4) countries which offer high returns on investment. The latter has become a feature of capital flight from Russia only since the late-1990s (Tikhomirov 2001).

During the 1990s, it was estimated that Russian capital flight totaled at least USD 150 bn. According to the European Commission (2004: 11), USD 245 bn is estimated to have flown from Russia during 1992-2002. Russia's FDI outflow (USD 18 bn during 1992-2002) is, therefore, less than 10% of the capital flight. However, due to the Russian economic boom of recent years and economic downturn in most other parts of the world, the capital flight has contracted. It decreased from 10% of the Russian GDP during 1998-2001 to a mere 0.6% in 2003 prior to the Yukos affair (Pelto et al. 2003: 6, 14; Vahtra/Liuhto 2004: 5, 11).

Geographical Destination

According to UNCTAD (2003b: 31), information on the structural patterns, such as the geographical destination of outward FDI from CEE, is scattered and has to be interpreted with care. However, outward FDI flows in the second half of the 1990s indicate that Russian investment activities are highly regionally concentrated; the main destination for Russian FDI was the EU15 with a share of 31%. The second major destination was CEE, including the countries of the Commonwealth of Independent States (CIS), with a share of 25% followed by North America with 23%. These three regions alone amount for nearly 80% of Russian outward FDI (calculation based on Kalotay 2003: 11-13).

Within the EU the main destination was Germany, covering between 1995 and 2001 with USD 1990 million more than half of Russian FDI outflows to the EU. By a wide margin Germany was followed by the Netherlands (USD 633 mn) and the UK (USD 532 mn). Other member countries did not play a major role as a destination for Russian FDI.

Before the EU enlargement in May 2004, the main destinations within the EU were still Germany with a Russian FDI stock of USD 920 mn (as of January 2003), and, more recently, France with a FDI stock of USD 390 mn (as of January 2004), followed by Austria (USD 385 mn as of January 2003) and Finland (USD 307 mn as of January 2003). Together they cover over 90% of Russia's outward FDI stock in the EU, amounting to USD 2,178 mn before the enlargement (Bundesbank 2004: 57; Vahtra/Liuhto 2004: 13).

Structure

The structure of the Russian outward FDI is characterized by the dominance of companies from the raw material sector, primarily oil and gas companies. According to UNCTAD (2004a: 74), more than half of the 15 leading outward investing companies in terms of new projects set up abroad were from the natural resources sector in 2002-2003 (namely Alrosa, Gazprom, Group Alliance, Itera Group, Lukoil, RusAl, UES, and Yukos).[2]

In the energy industry, in particular, Russian companies started to diversify their production base and access foreign markets by acquiring companies and establishing foreign affiliates. However, cross-border acquisitions of Russian firms tended to have a small volume–in the order of USD 200-300 mn. In 2004, the size of mergers and acquisitions by Russian firms rose (UNCTAD 2004a: 74).

Besides natural-resource-based firms, the list of the top 15 Russian investors includes three automotive producers, one IT company, one telecom operator, one insurance company and one food producer. The expansion of non-natural resource-based companies abroad is a recent phenomenon. However, during the past few years, these companies have been active, opening production facilities, representative offices and sales units abroad to tap new markets and seize new business opportunities (UNCTAD 2004a: 74).

GERMANY AS A DESTINATION OF RUSSIAN FDI

Since the mid-1980s, the FDI outflows from Germany have increased strongly but on the other side FDI inflows to Germany have vacillated and decreased since the mid-1990s (Deutsche Bundesbank 1997: 63). The re-unification of Germany in 1990 did not lead to a strong increase in FDI inflows to Germany. Foreign companies did not participate in large numbers in the privatization process of East German companies. As investment obstacles the German Central Bank identified the following issues: (1) bureaucratic over-regulation (red tape); (2) high taxes; (3) high wages; (4) short working hours; (5) inflexible labor market; (6) legal and organizational structures making merger and acquisitions difficult; and (7) the tiny number of German companies listed on the German stock exchange, in which capitalization is low in comparison to Germany's GDP (Deutsche Bundesbank 1997: 74-76).

However, Germany–itself the biggest market in Europe with 82 million people–is situated in the centre of a unified economic zone with around 450 million consumers, and is quite literally the hub of the EU. Today, more goods move through Germany than through any other European country because it shares land borders with nine countries and boasts major ports on both the North Sea and Baltic Sea. Germany has the infrastructure to exploit its geographical advantage; its infrastructure is among the most extensive and highly developed in the world (Invest-in-Germany Newsletter, No. 5, 2004: 2-3; Invest-in-Germany Newsletter, No. 3, 2004: 3).

As indicated by Table 2, the Russian presence in the German market was characterized by a small number of registered companies doing business in Germany. This number was even decreasing (in 2002 for methodological reasons). These companies did not generate much employment; their stable average is around 1,000 employees. However, after 1996 the averaged assets of the Russian companies increased steadily and nearly doubled in 2002 compared to 1994. The sales of the Russian companies in Germany have in general been developed in line with the German-Russian trade balance. The decrease in the years 2001 and 2002 despite high oil prices can be explained by the weak exchange rate of the US dollar against the euro. Raw materials, the major Russian export goods, are mainly paid in US dollars.

The Russian Embassy in Germany describes the level of Russian investment activities in the country as small; however, it counted around

TABLE 2. Characteristics of Russian Companies in Germany, 1994-2002

	1994	1995	1996	1997	1998	1999	2000	2001	2002
Number of affiliates[1]	62	59	57	55	57	46	42	41	27
Assets (EUR million)	4,806	4,090	3,375	3,375	3,579	4,000	4,000	4,400	4,000
Employment	1,000	1,000	1,000	1,000	1,000	1,000	1,000	1,000	1,000
Sales (EUR million)	3,068	3,221	4,295	4,755	3,886	4,700	6,600	5,300	4,800

Sources: UNCTAD 2004b: 33, 38, 43, 48. Figures for 2002 according to Deutsche Bundesbank 2004: 57; own calculations.
[1]Notes: Figure for 2002 without in Germany registered holding companies. Additionally, in 2002, the declaration limit for the value of assets of investment projects with foreign capital involvement to the German Central Bank was increased from EUR 0.5 mn to EUR 3.0 mn. This measure reduced the number of registered companies with foreign capital by around 4,600 firms. Simultaneously, the declaration limit for the asset value of investment projects with minority foreign capital involvement was reduced from EUR 5.0 mn to EUR 3.0 mn which increased the number of registered foreign companies by around 230 (Deutsche Bundesbank 2004: 5).

100 companies with Russian capital (Russian Embassy in Germany 2004). The number of companies mentioned by the Embassy far exceeds the German Central Bank's numbers. That might be an indication that the volume of the invested (and reported) capital has not yet reached the Bank's recording threshold of a half million euros. In 2002, this threshold was increased to three million, so that even fewer companies are recorded. It seems that there are many small businesses with Russian emigrant or Russian born ethnic German (Aussiedler) proprietors attracting Russian capital which are not statistically recorded by the German Central Bank or mentioned by the media.

Motives and Forms of Internationalization in Germany

Analyzing the motives of Russian investments in Germany resource seeking and efficiency seeking can be excluded. Germany is not a resource rich country and labor costs are high in international comparison.

The dominant motive for Russian companies to enter a foreign market is to open up possibilities for business. The companies strive for prominence in foreign markets and they try to achieve this without intermediaries because it is more profitable and reliable to do so without a middle man. Negative aspects of Russia's investment climate, such as high taxation as well as political and legal instability, which might ordinarily work as push factors, were not the dominant motives for outward FDI of older companies analyzed by Bulatov (2001). These ownership disadvantages might be more important for smaller start-up companies (Bulatov 2001: 186, 193).

Representation Offices/Marketing Subsidiaries

For market seeking purposes several Russian corporations established representation offices or marketing subsidiaries in Germany.

Wimm-Bill-Dann is the leading food producer in Russia. Since 1999, the company has been regularly exporting its juices and juice-based drinks to North America, Israel, Germany, the Netherlands and the UK through both its own distribution network and independent distributors. In line with the company's partnership practices, Wimm-Bill-Dann has established close co-operation with its importers across the world. In the second half of 2001, the company commenced its activities in new prospective directions: the setting up of Wimm-Bill-Dann Deutschland GmbH with residence in Berlin (Vahtra/Liuhto 2004: 71-72; company information). At this point, the company had already exported 3,000 tons of its fruit drinks to European markets–720 tons to Germany alone, which had a market share of around 25% (NewsBase, Agri Digest, 6 June 2001).

In September 2004, Wimm-Bill-Dann also obtained a license to export its dairy products to EU countries. The company is currently involved in negotiations with retail chains in Latvia, Lithuania and Germany regarding the possible supply of dairy products. The company is targeting large expatriate Russian communities in EU countries. These products are expected to have plenty of scope in EU markets where there are large numbers of expatriates willing to buy dairy products that remind them of home that simply cannot be purchased outside of Russia (company information). The items will also introduce Russian food products to German customers.

Large Russian corporations from the raw materials sector have also established a foothold in Germany. The titanium and magnesium producer VSMPO-Avisma established a fully-owned trading and marketing subsidiary in Germany to increase its presence in the European market (Vahtra/Liuhto 2004: 54). Through its German subsidiary Tirus GmbH, based in Frankfurt/Main, it also owns its US subsidiary Tirus US (Haflich 2000). In order to facilitate its exports, the aluminum company RusAl has founded a representative office in Düsseldorf, Germany (Vahtra/Liuhto 2004: 50).

In 2001, the financial corporation NIKoil established a representative office in Berlin to service the growing German need for financial advice in doing business with Russia. The company is already involved in a third of all business contracts signed between German and Russian companies (company information). In 2004, NIKoil was followed by Frankfurt/Main-based Risk Invest Deutschland AG which also provides financial services for Western investors in Russia.

Joint Ventures and Acquisitions

Market seeking in combination with strategic asset or capability seeking through joint ventures and acquisitions can be determined as the other main motives for the internationalization of Russian companies and their investment activities in Germany.

As early as 1991, the Russian car-maker AvtoVaz established the FerroVAZ joint venture together with MAN-Ferrostaal, which holds a 50% interest. The joint venture is registered in Essen and engaged in exports, imports and engineering. It employs 11 people and has company capital of around two million US dollars. The annual turnover amounts to around USD 31 mn. The main products which are imported are chemical products, ironmongery, mechanical handling equipment, metals, motor vehicles and hardware (company information).

The Russian glass producer Gus-Kristall, with a 250 year old tradition of glass production, bought the Glashütte Döbern in Brandenburg in 2002 after the German company ran into financial problems. This acquisition secured 110 jobs in Döbern and opened the door to Europe for the Russian company. While Gus-Kristall had no export activities in 1999, it exported around 12% of its production in 34 countries in 2003. At the German location Gus-Kristall plans to establish a Russian village to attract tourists as well as visitors to the production facilities (Funk 2004).

Russia's Gazprom nearly holds the monopoly on production, transport and export of natural gas. Gazprom has profited from the EU gas market liberalization initiatives by gaining access to the downstream business in Western Europe. To participate in the profitable downstream market, Gazprom has established joint venture marketing companies in nearly all the countries to which Russian natural gas is exported (see Table 3).

Germany is the world's second largest importer of natural gas and, therefore, the largest European gas market. Additionally, Gazprom is using Germany as an entry to the West European pipeline grid, as a hub for the transport of Russian gas to other European countries.

Strategic Partnership

Capability seeking through co-operation agreements or strategic partnerships is also a motive for the internationalization of Russian companies in Germany. The most prominent example is Gazprom.

The company is engaging in strategic partnerships with leading Western natural gas companies in order to gain access to new markets

TABLE 3. Gazprom's Joint Ventures in Germany

Company	Stake	Activity
Ditgaz	49%	Gas trading
Verbundnetz Gas	5%	Gas transportation and marketing
Wingas	35%	Gas transportation and storage
Wintershall Erdgas Handelshaus (WIEH)	50%	Only trader of Gazprom's exports until 2012
Zarubezhgaz	100%	Gas trading

Source: Heinrich 2003: 61.

and new sources of finance. It is a means of bringing in foreign companies that have their own access to loans at more affordable rates. In Germany, Gazprom is co-operating with Ruhrgas (E.ON group) and BASF/ Wintershall (Heinrich 2003: 59-60).

The co-operation with Ruhrgas–which has a market share of around 60% in Germany–helped Gazprom to increase its access to the West European gas market and to prepare for the partial liberalization of the EU gas market. The partnership with Ruhrgas started in 1970, when the first supply contract between the Soviet Union and Ruhrgas was signed. In the period from 1973 to 1997, Soviet, respectively Russian, natural gas sales to Ruhrgas amounted to a total of 355 billion cubic meters, worth around USD 33 bn (at current prices). Until the year 2020, an additional 370 billion cubic meters, worth USD 36 bn, are to be delivered according to present contracts. By the end of 2003, Ruhrgas held a stake of six per cent in Gazprom and a seat on the company board (NewsBase, FSU Oil & Gas Monitor, No. 20, 19 May 2004). The two companies are also realizing joint investment projects in CEE.

In 1989, Gazprom began to look for new business opportunities in the West European downstream sector. However, Ruhrgas seemed to be unwilling to grant its Russian partner access to that profitable part of the gas market. As a result, Gazprom signed a co-operation agreement with Wintershall–a subsidiary of BASF and one of the main competitors of Ruhrgas in the German natural gas market. The agreement includes the joint marketing of Russian natural gas through the joint venture Wingas, as well as the joint planning and construction of gas pipelines and storage facilities in Germany and in the neighboring countries. The resulting tensions with Ruhrgas eased only very slowly. The co-operation with Wintershall offers Gazprom lasting access to the West European gas supply system in the downstream sector. In March 1999, Gazprom formed a strategic alliance with BASF for exploiting oil and gas in Russia.

In June 2004, the ZukunftsAgentur Brandenburg (ZAB) and the Russian company BIOMAC Innovation signed a cooperation agreement. ZAB and BIOMAC are organizing and coordinating international technology projects between German and Russian companies in the area of biotechnology and pharmaceutics (life sciences), environmental and energy technology as well as optical and laser technology (ZAB, press release, http://www.zab-brandenburg.de/deutsch/presse/12250.htm).

BIOMAC has–together with ZAB–established a German-Russian consulting group which provides professional consulting services in marketing, analysis and partnership between Russian and German enterprises in the high-tech sphere (biotechnology, environment protection, energy, laser optics technique). BIOMAC offers (1) technological research on request of the foreign partners, (2) international matching of partners and implementation of joint ventures, (3) the finding of investors for Russian projects, (4) organization of seminars and educational conferences, and (5) presentations at trade fairs and exhibitions.

BIOMAC Innovations was established in 2001 in Moscow with the purpose of fostering the Russian innovation program 'Biotechnology for medicine and agro-industrial complex' on the basis of the cooperation agreement among the Russian ministries of industry and sciences, public health, agriculture and education. It is a product of a Public-Private Partnership, co-owned by the Russian Ministries of Science and Industry and several private companies.

The mission of BIOMAC is to create an effective infrastructure for the implementation and adaptation of advanced know-how in biotechnology. The company takes part in the realization of these projects from the idea stage to the commercial production stage. It already cooperates with leading Finnish and French innovative organizations (science parks, funds, business-incubators).

Capital Flight

Stability seeking is another notable motive for Russian corporations to go abroad. Among the developed Western countries reported to host significant amounts of Russian flight capital was Germany, which additionally had large Russian-speaking communities. In 1999, in only one area of Germany, the Rhine region, there were more than 50 active Russian real estate and foreign trade firms. Local authorities estimated that the illegal turnover of Russian capital in this region amounted to USD 150 mn a week (Tikhomirov 2001).

Dr. Arzinger gave a presentation on his experiences with Russian investment behavior in Germany. He mentioned that in the early 1990s many Russian businessmen just transferred their capital to their second place of residence. In the last few years, Arzinger noticed a more serious interest in using Germany as a basis for business operations in the European market. This behavior might be an explanation for the small number of companies about which information is available.

CONCLUSION

As an old EU member state, Germany's reluctance to host Russian investments is much smaller than in the new member countries due to different historical experiences (cf. Heinrich 2004). Since the mid-1970s, the Soviet Union (and later the Russian Federation) has established itself as a reliable trading partner of strategic important energy sources, primarily natural gas. Thus, Gazprom's gains in establishing marketing and transport subsidiaries as well as getting access to the downstream market in Germany were welcomed. The Russian natural gas giant was able to establish wholly-owned subsidiaries and joint ventures with German partners.

However, there are some basic difficulties for other Russian companies in acquiring stakes in German or–more generally–in companies in old EU member states. Markets are highly competitive and dominated by capital-scraping western companies and, therefore, lucrative acquisitions often require much more capital than privatization auctions in CEE. Additionally, Russian companies are not–at least not in an unknown business environment–at the competitive edge. The competitiveness might not be so important for companies from the raw materials sector because of their huge resource base, which make them attractive for a partnership. This might explain why Russian companies have established mostly representative offices and marketing subsidiaries in Germany.

Another reason might be grounded in the structure of the internationalizing companies (see Table 4). The Russian economy is dominated by the raw material sector, as is the trade and outward FDI structure. Oil and gas companies dominate internationalization of Russian firms followed by companies from the metals sector. The motives for internationalization of Russian companies of the raw materials sector are more resource seeking than market seeking. Therefore, these companies have established mostly only representational offices in Germany to foster

TABLE 4. A Summary of Findings

Structure of internationalization	• numerical dominance of small companies
	• large companies belong mostly to the raw materials sector
	• mostly unspecific investment activities through representative offices or marketing subsidiaries
	• most significant and specific investment was made by Gazprom
Motives of internationalization	• main motive is market seeking
	• strategic asset and capability seeking is more seldom
	• large number of small firms might be an indication of capital flight (motive: stability seeking)

their exports. Market seeking also includes macroeconomic and macro-organizational policies as pursued by host governments, like market prices for exported goods (price liberalization), which explains Russia's trade structure with Germany (cf. Dunning 1998: 53).

Nevertheless, the Russian machinery, automotive and financial corporations as well as food and glass producers and IT companies have notably expanded their international operations during the past years. These companies provide an example of an active market-seeking strategy. They have also established representative offices in Germany.

Only a small number of Russian corporations is involved in more specific investments in Germany, driven by the motive of strategic asset and capability seeking. One example is Gazprom, which depends on long-lasting trade contracts because Russian natural gas is transported via pipelines only. Therefore, it is interested in tighter relationships with its business partners, first of all in Germany, which is its hub to the whole of Western Europe. BIOMAC is also attempting to establish a tight connection between the German and Russian technology sector to integrate Russia and its experts and institutes into the European scientific community.

Small businesses seem to dominate the investment activities in number in Germany. Larger, export-orientated Russian companies use Germany as a window to Europe–primarily to the old EU member states–by using its technological and intellectual infrastructure.

NOTES

1. According to IMF and OECD recommendations, direct investment is the category of international investment that reflects the objective of a resident entity in one economy (direct investor) of establishing a lasting interest in an enterprise resident in another economy.
2. Due to its connections to former Gazprom managers, UNCTAD counts Itera Group as a Russian corporation, although its headquarter, is in the USA.

REFERENCES

Bruggmann, Mathias (2003) Russische IT-Firmen profitieren von der weltweiten Wirtschaftskrise. Handelsblatt, 2 September.

Buckley, Peter J. (1988) Foreign Investment: The Motives, in Brooke, Michael Z./Peter J. Buckley (eds), Handbook of International Trade. Macmillan: London, pp. 203-212.

Bulatov, Alexander S. (2001) Russian Direct Investment Abroad: History, Motives, Finance, Control and Planning. Economies of Planning, Vol. 34, pp. 179-194.

Deutsche Bundesbank (1997) Entwicklung und Bestimmungsgründe grenzüberschreitender Direktinvestitionen. Monatsberichte, August, pp. 63-82.

Deutsche Bundesbank (2004) Kapitalverflechtung mit dem Ausland. Deutsche Bundesbank: Frankfurt/Main (Statistische Sonderveröffentlichung 10).

Dunning, John H. (1980) Towards an Eclectic Theory of International Production: Some Empirical Tests. Journal of International Business Studies, Vol. 11, No. 1, pp. 9-31.

Dunning, John H. (1988) The Eclectic Paradigm of International Production: A Restatement and Some Possible Extensions. Journal of International Business Studies, Vol. 19, No. 1, pp. 1-31.

Dunning, John H. (1993) Multinational Enterprises and the Global Economy. Addison-Wesley: Wokingham, Berks.

Dunning, John H. (1998) Location and the Multinational Enterprise. A Neglected Factor? Journal of International Business Studies, Vol. 29, No. 1, pp. 45-66.

European Commission (2004) Communication from the Commission to the Council and the European Parliament on Relations with Russia, COM(2004) 106. EC: Brussels.

Funk, Viktor (2004) Ein kleines russisches Wirtschaftswunder. DW-RADIO, 1 April.

Goskomstat Rossii (2003a) Rossiya i strany-chleny evropeickogo soyuza 2003. Goskomstat: Moscow.

Goskomstat Rossii (2003b) Rossiiskii statisticheckii ezhegodnik 2003. Goskomstat: Moscow.

Götz, Roland/Meier, Christian (2001) German-Russian Economic Relations. Options for German-Russian Economic Relations. SWP: Berlin.

Haflich, Frank (2000) Russian Titanium Producer Eyeing US. American Metal Market, 21 September.

Heinrich, Andreas (2003) Internationalisation of Russia's Gazprom. Journal for East European Management Studies, Vol. 8, No. 1, pp. 46-66.

Heinrich, Andreas (2004) EU Enlargement and the Challenges for the Internationalization of Companies from Central and Eastern Europe: Insiders and Outsiders in the Energy Sector. Paper prepared for the conference "New Europe 2020: Visions and Strategies for Wider Europe," Turku, Finland, 27-28 August 2004.

Hymer, Stephen H. (1976) The International Operations of National Firms: A Study of Foreign Direct Investment. MIT Press: Cambridge, MA.

Kalotay, Kálmán (2003) Outward Foreign Direct Investment from Economies in Transition in the Global Context. Journal for East European Management Studies, Vol. 8, No. 1, pp. 6-24.

Liuhto, Kari/Jumpponen, Jari (2003) Russian Corporations and Banks Abroad. Journal for East European Management Studies, Vol. 8, No. 1, pp. 26-45.

Ost-Ausschuss der deutschen Wirtschaft (2004) Positionspapier: Einschätzung der deutsch-russischen Wirtschaftsbeziehungen. OA: Berlin.

Pelto, Elina/Vahtra, Peeter/Liuhto, Kari (2003) Cyp-Rus Investment Flows to Central and Eastern Europe. Russia's Direct and Indirect Investments via Cyprus to CEE. Pan-European Institute: Turku.

Tikhomirov, Vladimir (2001) Capital Flight: Causes, Consequences and Counter-Measures. In: Segbers, Klaus (ed.): Explaining Post-Soviet Patchworks. Vol. 2: Pathways from the Past to the Global. Ashgate: Aldershot, pp. 251-280.

UNCTAD (2003) World Investment Directory, Volume VIII: Central and Eastern Europe. United Nations: New York.

UNCTAD (2004a) World Investment Report 2004. The Shift Towards Services. United Nations: New York.

UNCTAD (2004b) Country Portrait Germany. United Nations: New York.

Vahtra, Peeter/Liuhto, Kari (2004) Expansion or Exodus? Foreign Operations of Russia's Largest Corporations. Pan-European Institute: Turku.

Williamson, Oliver E. (1975) Markets and Hierarchies, Analysis and Antitrust Implications: A Study in the Economics of Internal Organizations. Free Press: New York.

WTO (2004) International Trade Statistics 2004. WTO: Geneva.

Russia's Foreign Direct Investments in New EU Member States: The Case of the Baltic States

Kaarel Kilvits
Alari Purju
Sirje Pädam

SUMMARY. Russia's FDI in the Baltic States has been increasing over the last two to three years. The EU membership of the Baltic States and access to the EU market, accompanied by available sources for investment as a result of economic growth in Russia, have been the main reasons for that increase. At the same time, FDI from Russia have been met with suspicion in the Baltic States. Two main reasons for trying to avoid Russian investments have been the fear of losing control over the vital aspects of the economy and sometimes unclear sources of investment. A case study depicts problems and developments in an Estonian natural gas company with Russia's FDI, Eesti Gaas. *[Article copies available for a fee from The Haworth Document Delivery Service: 1-800-HAWORTH. E-mail address: <docdelivery@haworthpress.com> Website: <http://www.HaworthPress.com> © 2005 by The Haworth Press, Inc. All rights reserved.]*

Kaarel Kilvits is Professor of Economic Policy and Head of Public Economy Department, Tallinn University of Technology, Faculty of Economics and Business Administration. Alari Purju is Professor of Economics, Estonian Business School and Research Associate, Tallinn University of Technology. Sirje Pädam is PhD Candidate and Research Associate, Tallinn University of Technology and Research Associate, Inregia AB.

[Haworth co-indexing entry note]: "Russia's Foreign Direct Investments in New EU Member States: The Case of the Baltic States." Kilvits, Kaarel, Alari Purju, and Sirje Pädam. Co-published simultaneously in *Journal of East-West Business* (The Haworth Press, Inc.) Vol. 11, No. 3/4, 2005, pp. 61-73; and: *Expansion or Exodus: Why Do Russian Corporations Invest Abroad?* (ed: Kari Liuhto) The Haworth Press, Inc., 2005, pp. 61-73. Single or multiple copies of this article are available for a fee from The Haworth Document Delivery Service [1-800-HAWORTH, 9:00 a.m. - 5:00 p.m. (EST). E-mail address: docdelivery@haworthpress.com].

Available online at http://www.haworthpress.com/web/JEB

doi:10.1300/J097v11n03_05

KEYWORDS. Russian investments in the Baltic States, Eesti Gaas

INTRODUCTION

The Baltic States regained independence from the Soviet Union in 1991. A strong factor driving their politics and economies has been integration with the West and drifting away from Russia. That policy paid off in the membership of the European Union and the NATO. Foreign direct investments from the EU and USA have been seen as an important factor of the integration process due to additional financial resources for investment and for making modern technologies available. The politicians in the Baltic States observed the potential investments not only in terms of their economic value but also for their political impact. In the light of candidacy for the EU and NATO membership it was considered important that priority should be given to investments from the EU and USA. Until the mid-1990s, the majority of the FDI went into privatized companies. As politicians constituted a major part of the boards of privatization agencies it was quite easy to realize those political preferences. Afterwards the situation changed because more greenfield investments were made and investment decisions were made by private companies.

At the same time, the relationship with Russia was not without problems. The political relationships of Estonia and Latvia with Russia were damaged by the fact that the Russian Parliament did not ratify the border agreement. The formal cause, as it was presented by the Russian side, has been poor treatment of Russian speaking minorities in those countries.[1] That has been an obstacle to signing trade agreements. Estonia and Latvia did not have the status of the Most Favored Nation (MFN), which caused double tariffs on exports from those countries to Russia. That regime was adopted only together with the EU membership of the Baltic States in May 2004, within the framework of political agreements between the EU and Russia.[2]

Lithuania did not have such an obstacle, partly due to the much smaller proportion of the Russian-speaking minority.[3] A bilateral trade agreement between Lithuania and Russia was signed in November 1993 and came into force in 1995, giving both countries the MFN status. That meant lower customs tariffs for the Lithuanian exports to Russia in comparison with Estonia and Latvia.

The economies of the Baltic States could see economic advantages in linkages with Russia. The primary energy resources and raw materials from Russia are important for the Baltic States. The Baltic Sea ports have been an important transit channel for Russian exports to the EU and other countries. Under these circumstances, investments that accompany and support that trade might be a reasonable economic step. However, FDI from Russia have been met with suspicion in the Baltic States. The two main reasons for trying to avoid Russian investments have been the fear of losing control over the vital aspects of the economy and sometimes unclear source of investment.

The political and economic development in Russia has supported those fears. Russia has been recently transformed from an economy with steadily declining output and chronic macroeconomic instability to a dynamic economy with macroeconomic stability. The concentration of power into hands of the central government and an increasing state control over the economy is another aspect of recent changes in Russia.

The article covers the main trends of FDI from Russia to the Baltic States. The official statistical figures will be the main source of information. Several other countries have been considered as a secondary source of investment from Russia when subsidiaries of Russian companies registered there invested into the Baltic States. The paper ends with a case study of the natural gas transportation and distribution company *Eesti Gaas*.

RUSSIA'S OUTWARD FDI IN THE BALTIC STATES: A STATISTICAL OVERVIEW

Estonia and Latvia differ from Lithuania, as they received a considerable amount of Russia's FDI early in the 1990s. In 1994, FDI inflow from Russia made up 15% of Estonia's inward FDI. However, after 1994 Russia's FDI into Estonia did not increase until 1999. In Latvia, the Russian FDI stock peaked in 1995 when it was close to 19% of the total stock of foreign direct investments into Latvia. These differences in FDI inflows most probably mirror the timing and ideology of privatization (Frydman et al., 1995). Judging from the data on the stock of Russia's direct investments, all three Baltic economies have experienced an increase in Russia's direct investments over the past two to three years. The most significant growth of Russia's investments concerns Lithuania (see Figure 1).

Russia's outward foreign direct investments affect mostly large enterprises in the sector of natural resources or transportation (*World Investment Directory*, 2003). This structure is detectable also in the Baltic States, as Russian investments to a substantial degree comprise investments into the energy sector and transit shipment infrastruc-

FIGURE 1. Russia's FDI Stock in the Baltic States (Left Axis: USD Million; Right Axis: Russia as Percentages of Total Stock)

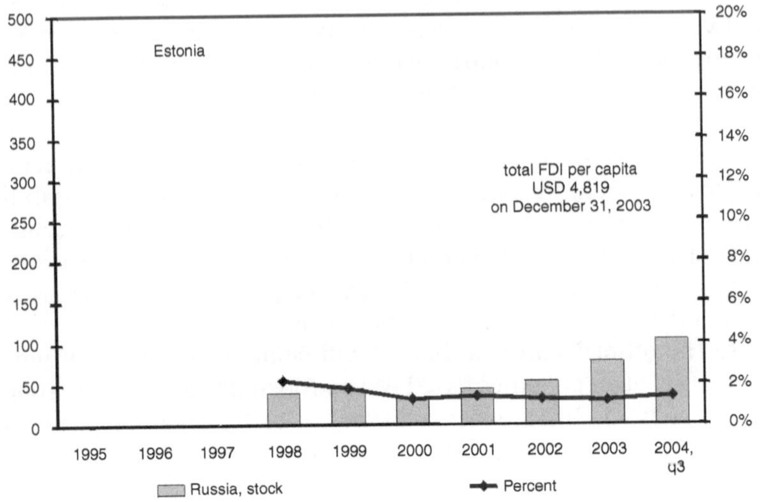

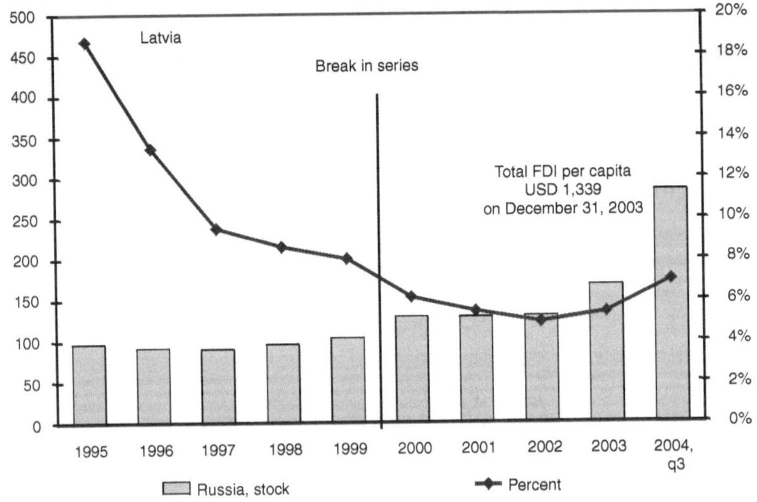

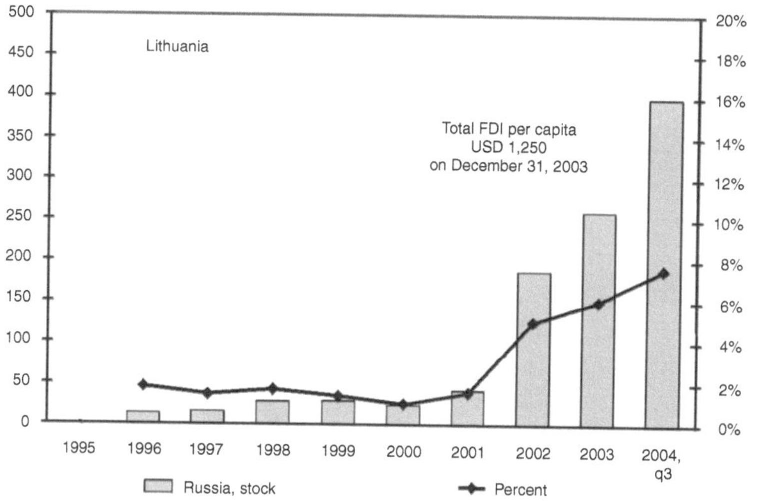

Sources: Authors' calculations, the Bank of Estonia, *www.eestipank.info*, Statistical Office of Latvia, the Central Bank of Latvia and the Central Bank of Lithuania.

ture.[4] A significant part of Russia's FDI stock into Lithuania involved manufacturing industry (at the end of September 2004), which was mostly spent on refining petroleum. Approximately 30% had been invested in the energy sector and 6% in services. About half of the service sector investments involved trade and repairs, a somewhat smaller share had been provided to transport and communications.

Russia's investments accounted for 5% of the Latvian FDI stock at the end of 2003 (see Table 1). The equivalent figure for Lithuania was 6%. In the Estonian economy, Russia's investments made up only 1% of the stock of FDI. These figures suggest a low penetration rate of Russian foreign direct investments in the Baltic countries. However, it is generally believed and shown by different sources of information that the economic influence of Russia is stronger. In the case of Estonia, experts estimate that Russian investments make up 5-7% of the stock of FDI, several times more than the official figure. The same is true in Latvia and Lithuania.[5]

CASE STUDY: EESTI GAAS

The ownership structures of the gas companies in the Baltic States and Finland are quite similar. The main supplier is a minor shareholder

TABLE 1. Russia as a Foreign Investor and Trade Partner for the Baltic States (Russia's Share in Percent)

	FDI stock			Imports			Exports		
	Estonia	Latvia	Lithua-nia	Estonia	Latvia	Lithua-nia	Estonia	Latvia	Lithua-nia
2000	1.2	6.1	1.0	8.5	11.6	27.2	2.4	4.2	6.1
2003	1.2	5.4	6.0	8.6	8.7	22.7	3.9	5.4	8.9

Note: Trade according to special trading system.
Sources: Central Banks and the Foreign Trade–Estonia, Latvia, Lithuania, 2001, 2003.

together with a large international Western company who provides know-how, financial resources for restructuring and access to already existing or perspective networks. We describe here the developments of *Eesti Gaas*, but there are a lot of similarities also in all the other gas companies in the Baltic States. The main sources of information for the case study were annual reports of the gas companies and an interview with advisor to *Eesti Gaas*, Arvi Hamburg (see Table 2).

The state enterprise *Eesti Gaas* was founded in 1990. State enterprise was an intermediary form of ownership in order to remove enterprises from direct ministry control when waiting for privatization. *Eesti Gaas* was the first enterprise in the energy sector that was transformed into a state enterprise. There are two circumstances that explain why *Eesti Gaas* was the first. The ministry in Moscow disappeared as a result of administrative reforms in Moscow and the local companies gained independence. The second factor is that Aarne Saar, who still is the managing director of *Eesti Gaas*, was a strong leader. In 1992, the State Enterprise *Eesti Gaas* was ready for privatization. The actual privatization was carried out by the then Ministry of Industry and Power Engineering, not the Estonian Privatization Agency.

It was clear from the start that the strategy was to find a strategic investor and to sell 100% of the shares to private owners. *Gaz de France* was an interested buyer in the beginning, but when the first shares were sold in 1994 the firm was not among the investors. During the first wave of privatization, *Gazprom* acquired 30% and *Ruhrgas* 15% of the shares and the Estonian State kept a 39% stake of *Eesti Gaas*. The second wave of privatization took place in 1996-1999, during which the Estonian state sold all its shares. In 1996, discussions began about selling some 20% of the state shares of which one part would be sold to a strategic investor and the rest to the public for privatization vouchers.

TABLE 2. The Ownership Structure of Gas Companies in Lithuania, Latvia, Estonia and Finland (Percent)

Name of the company	Lithuania: Lietuvos Dujos	Latvia: Latvijas Gaze	Estonia: Eesti Gaas	Finland: Gasum
OAO Gazprom	37.1	25.0	37.0	25.0
E.ON Ruhrgas International AG	38.9	47.1	33.6	20.0
Itera Latvija		25.0	9.7	
Fortum			17.7	31.0
State ownership	17.7			24.0
Other shareholders	6.3	2.8	1.9	

Source: Enterprise information from annual reports 2003 and homepages accessed in January 2005.

However, it took time to agree about the sales due to the different views between the two foreign owners of *Eesti Gaas*. *Ruhrgas* was interested in increasing its share, but not *Gazprom*. In December 1996, the Estonian Privatization Agency decided to offer 29% of the shares of *Eesti Gaas* for sales: 12% to the public for privatization vouchers and 17% as pre-emptive rights to *Gazprom* and *Ruhrgas*, the remaining 10% was kept by the Estonian State until a strategic investor was found. *Ruhrgas* increased their share to 21%. *Gazprom* intended to use its pre-emptive right in order to increase the share to 41%. At the end of September 1998, Finnish *Neste* (later *Fortum*) bought the Estonian state shares and became the holder of 10% of *Eesti Gaas*. By this time the Estonian state still owned 11% of the shares that were intended for *Gazprom*.

However, in November 1998, it was decided that *Ruhrgas* would be given the right to buy the remaining part of state ownership because *Gazprom* was not allowed to make any foreign investments due to the difficult economic situation during the aftermaths of the Russian crises. In January 1999, the deal was settled. *Ruhrgas* became the owner of 32%, *Gazprom* retained 30% and *Neste* 10%. Small shareholders owned 27%. Two months later, in March 1999, *Itera Latvija* acquired almost 10% of *Eesti Gaas* by buying shares from the investment fund Baltic Republics Fund. Since then three of the owners–*Gazprom, Ruhrgas* and *Fortum*–have increased their shares by buying from small shareholders (Annual Reports of Eesti Gaas, 1996-2003).

As a contrast to other privatization cases there was no wish from *Gazprom* to become a majority owner. During the first wave of the privatization process, the director of *Levtransgaz* (*Levtransgaz* is a 100% owned subsidiary of *Gazprom*) visited Estonia as a representative for *Gazprom*. His view was that *Gazprom* should be in the circle of owners, but should have a role of learning and showing. After the first wave of privatization there were three owners with almost equal control (*Gazprom*, *Ruhrgas* and the Estonian State).

The two large private owners have divided the areas of responsibility: *Gazprom* is responsible for purchases and *Ruhrgas* for distribution and sales. Currently there is no permanent presence of either company in Estonia. Until 1997, representatives from both *Gazprom* and *Ruhrgas* belonged to the company management. However, in Latvia and Lithuania there are still representatives from *Gazprom* and *Ruhrgas* in the firm management. But in the Estonian case, owners have seen no need to be located in Estonia because as owners they have automatic access to information. The owner influence is channeled via the board of directors. Ever since the beginning, the decisions of the board have been based on consensus, first between the three large owners and later between the five large owners.

There have been discussions among the new owners of *Ruhrgas* (*Ruhrgas* was taken over by *E.ON* in 2003) to establish a representation in Estonia.[6] If *E.ON* opens a representation, it is very probable that also *Gazprom* creates its presence. Although different companies, there is cross ownership between *E.ON Ruhrgas* and *Gazprom*. In December 1998, *Ruhrgas* acquired a 3% stake in *OAO Gazprom*. After that *Ruhrgas* has increased its investment several times and currently holds 6% of the shares in *Gazprom* either directly or indirectly. Since 2000, the Chairman of the Board of *Ruhrgas,* Dr. Burckhard Bergmann, is the first and still the sole foreign representative to be elected into the Board of Directors of *Gazprom* (Annual Reports of E.ON Ruhrgas and Gazprom, 2003).

A critical issue for gas companies is how to secure supplies. Uncertainty is due either to fluctuations in demand or uncertain supply. Owing to the underground natural gas storage in Incukalns, Latvia, the supplies to Estonia are not vulnerable against short-term interruptions in supplies from Russia. Estonia also prepares for high demand periods by storing natural gas for the winter period in the Incukalns natural gas storage area. If the supplies from Russia fail, then Estonia will be provided with supplies from Incukalns for one year.

During the history of *Eesti Gaas*, Estonia has signed long-term, usually 5-year agreements with *Gazprom*. The current agreement was signed in 2000 and will be renegotiated in 2006. The content of the agreement includes the conditions of supply and clauses about consequences if there is interruption. The price consists of two parts: a base price and a fluctuating part. The latter varies with the world market price of oil. When setting the price level, *Gazprom* follows the prices of consumer goods and of Estonian shale oil. Sales prices also include costs of pipeline transport and storage costs paid to Incukalns.

Households in Estonia pay less for natural gas than households in Germany, which partly depends on shorter distance of pipeline distribution. However, Estonian households also pay less than Finnish households, because *Gazprom* takes into consideration the purchasing power. For large customers, making up 96% of the sales, *Eesti Gaas* offers two contract alternatives: (a) the price is pegged to the oil prices of the past 6 months, or (b) the price is pegged to the oil price of the previous month. Only 4% of the sales are to household customers whose price is fixed and accepted by the Estonian Energy Inspection. Under the current price construction, *Eesti Gaas* takes a risk that the price contracts may lead to a situation where revenues from gas sales are smaller than the purchasing costs. However, owing to increasing oil prices in recent years, the annual revenues have been about one billion EEK, the profit 100 million and investments in the range of 70-80 million.

Imports of natural gas have been liberalized. There are two requirements for those who wish to become importers: (1) measurability on the border and (2) there must be a contract with *Eesti Gaas,* i.e., the body responsible for the system. Currently there are two gas importers in Estonia–*Eesti Gaas* and *Nitrofert*. The latter produces fertilizers from natural gas.

Perhaps one could argue that it was not inescapable to include *Gazprom* among the owners of *Eesti Gaas*. But on the other hand, it is favorable. So far, the corporate culture of *Gazprom* has been that of a business organization. Because of the merger with *Rosneft* (100% state ownership), the share of Russian state ownership in *Gazprom* has increased. In 2005, the Russian State has announced that it will increase its share in *Gazprom* from 38% to 51%. *Gazprom* may therefore begin to act more like a Russian state enterprise. However, another political factor may influence Estonia more. Russia and the European Union are involved in an energy dialogue. Prices of energy are on the agenda and one issue under discussion is the price of natural gas. It is not improbable that Russia and the EU will agree that the price of natural gas will be equal throughout Europe.

Estonia and *Eesti Gaas* are not involved in the plans to build the Nordic Gas Pipeline, but the owners of *Eesti Gaas* are. The realization of the new gas pipeline project has been decided on the highest political level between the EU and Russia who signed an energy agreement in 2003. The agreement foresees a uniform distribution system in Europe and aims at security of supplies. The project is mainly political, because the market potential is small for those areas which will receive gas via the new pipeline. According to the plans, the new pipeline will run on the bottom of the Baltic Sea from Vyborg to Rostock. However, there are also plans to build a gas pipeline between Finland and Estonia. A feasibility study was initiated in late 2001. The project was launched by the Finns and involves a 90-kilometer gas pipeline under the Gulf of Finland. In future, the Finnish-Estonian pipeline can be connected to the Nordic gas pipeline.

The plan is that the Finnish partner will build the pipeline to the Estonian coastline. The Estonian responsibility begins from the first compressor station on the Estonian soil. *Gasum*, the Finnish gas company, points out that a pipeline connection between Finland and Estonia will pave the way for using Latvia's underground gas storage facilities for the benefit of Finnish needs (Chief executive officer's review in Gasum's Annual Report, 2003).

The current trend of water and energy companies is diversification. Water and sewage and heat distribution enterprises become involved in gas sales. For *Eesti Gaas* the diversification trend implies a need to get involved in other businesses than natural gas. In the future, *Eesti Gaas* may be one of 30 companies that sell gas in Estonia. In the Baltic market, a new entity–*Baltic Connector*–will be established as a result of an agreement between the gas companies in Estonia, Latvia, Finland, Russia and Lithuania (Lithuania probably not in the first wave because of Kaliningrad) to co-operate in gas transportation.

In the case of *Eesti Gaas,* the Russian investor has acted as a business partner, which may be due to various circumstances. The most obvious one is that *Gazprom's* corporate culture is business-oriented. However, there are other explanations connected to Estonia's role in the gas market. Comparing *Eesti Gaas* with *Mazeikiu Nafta,* or the Baltic companies and ports forwarding Russian transit shipments, it becomes evident that Estonia does not have a strategic role in the gas market. Instead Estonia represents a small sales market, since there is no transhipment of gas and only little refinement. These circumstances can be expected to continue in the future. The future markets in Germany and other countries in the European mainland will be reached via the Nordic Gas pipeline that will be built on the sea bottom between Vyborg and Rostock. Another explanation why gas has not been used as a political tool is that a cut in the supplies takes effect only after a time lag, which makes such threats relatively inefficient.

Recent changes in the ownership of *Eesti Gaas* point at two directions. The fact that both *E.ON Ruhrgas* and *Gazprom* have become diversified–*Ruhrgas* towards electricity and water, and *Gazprom* towards oil–will be significant for the new challenges of diversification lying ahead of *Eesti Gaas*. The know-how for entering the business of water, sewage and heating can be acquired internally. However, the increase in state ownership in *Gazprom* may affect *Eesti Gaas* in another way if the corporate culture of *Gazprom* changes, making *Gazprom* an owner, which to a larger degree takes political matters into account.

CONCLUSIONS

A strong factor driving the Baltic States' politics and economies has been integration with the West and drifting away from Russia. The FDI from the EU and USA have been seen as an important factor of integration, due to additional financial resources for investment and making modern technologies available.

The primary energy resources and raw materials from Russia are important for the Baltic States. The investments that accompany and support that trade could be a reasonable economic step. At the same time, FDI from Russia has been met with suspicion in the Baltic States. The two main reasons for trying to avoid Russian investments have been the fear of losing control over the vital aspects of the economy and sometimes an unclear source of investments.

The share of Russia's foreign direct investment stock was 5% in Latvia, 6% in Lithuania and 1% in Estonia of the total stock of FDI. These figures suggest a low penetration rate of Russian foreign direct investments in the Baltic countries. According to indirect estimates, the amount of FDI with Russia's background is larger, up to 3-4 times the official figures.

Russia's outward foreign direct investments concern mostly large enterprises in the sector of natural resources and transportation. This structure is detectable also in the Baltic economies, as Russian investments to a substantial degree comprise investments into the energy sector and transit shipment infrastructure.

The gas companies in the Baltic States and Finland are one example of FDI from Russia. The main supplier, *Gazprom,* has been a minor shareholder together with a large international Western company, providing know-how, financial resources for restructuring and access to already existing or future networks.

The Russian investor has acted as a business partner in the case of *Eesti Gaas*, which can be explained by different circumstances. *Gazprom's* corporate culture is business oriented. There are also other explanations connected to Estonia's role in the gas market. Comparing *Eesti Gaas* with *Mazeikiu Nafta,* or the Baltic companies and ports forwarding Russian transit shipments, it becomes evident that Estonia does not have a strategic role in the gas market. The supplies to Estonia are not vulnerable to short-term interruptions in supplies from Russia due to the underground natural gas storage in Incukalns, Latvia.

Russia's FDI into the Baltic States can be considered as a feature of internationalization of economies in the Baltic Sea region. A possible linkage to power politics and government interventions through FDI depends on the future political and economic developments in the region, Russia's development being the main factor.

NOTES

1. The EU membership of Estonia and Latvia meant that treatment of minorities should meet the requirements fixed as one of the so-called Copenhagen criteria.

2. The EU-Russian relations are based on the EU-Russia Partnership and Cooperation Agreement (PCA). The PCA was negotiated in 1993, signed in 1994, and finally came into force in 1997. The PCA determines the main areas for cooperation, the mechanisms of political dialogue and regulates economic relations. The EU extended the PCA to all new EU members and expected the same position of Russia assuming that the PCA would automatically widen also to the new members of the EU. However, just before the enlargement, in the last days of April 2004, Russia demonstrated its unwillingness to accept that position. During the last minute negotiations, the EU and Russia managed to agree on several compromise decisions, which included reduction of tariffs on the sensitive goods to Russia, increase of quotas for the Russian exports of steel, introduced a transition period for anti-dumping regime in Central and Eastern Europe, increased quotas for nuclear materials from the acceding countries and created a free transit of goods, including energy, between Kaliningrad and the Russian mainland (EU and Russia confirm the extension of the PCA . . ., 2004).

3. The proportion of Russians in all population was 29% in Latvia, 26% in Estonia and 6% in Lithuania at the beginning of 2003 (Estonia, Latvia, Lithuania in Figures, 2004).

4. For more details, see Vahtra and Liuhto (2004) and Vahtra and Lorentz (2004).

5. For example, one of the largest enterprises in Lithuania, Mazeikiu Oil, is partly owned by Yukos in Dutch registered subsidiary. The Swiss subsidiary of Yukos has been the main intermediary for Mazeikiu Oil sales to Western Europe. See Lithuania (2004), Estonia (2004), Latvia (2004), Zashev (2004).

6. In March 2003, *Ruhrgas* was taken over by the energy group *E.ON*, one of the largest privately owned energy companies with 35 million customers in the fields of electricity, gas and water. The owners of *E.ON* are insurance companies, banks, financial enterprises, investment funds and the public. German owners dominate and about 50% of the ownership is foreign. American capital owns 17% of *E.ON*.

REFERENCES

Annual Report of Gazprom (2003).
Annual Report of Gasum (2003).
Annual Reports of Eesti Gaas (1996-2003).
Central Bank of Russia (2005): *www.cbr.ru/eng/statistics.*
EIU (2004): Estonia, Country Report, Economist Intelligence Unit, London.
EIU (2004): Latvia, Country Report, Economist Intelligence Unit, London.
EIU (2004): Lithuania, Country Report, Economist Intelligence Unit, London.
Estonia, Latvia, Lithuania. Foreign Trade 2003 (2004): Riga, Statistics Latvia.
Estonia, Latvia, Lithuania. Foreign Trade 2001 (2002): Riga, Statistics Latvia.
Estonia, Latvia, Lithuania in Figures (2004): Tallinn, Statistical Office of Estonia.
Estonian Statistics, No.8 (2004), Tallinn, Statistical Office of Estonia.
EU and Russia Confirm the Extension of the PCA to the Enlarged EU (2004): IP/04/549, Brussels, 27 April.
Frydman, R., Rapaczynski, A., Earl, J. et al., ed. (1995): The Privatisation Process in Russia, Ukraine and the Baltic States, London, Central European University Press.
Quarterly Bulletin of Balance of Payments of the Republic of Lithuania (2000, 2001, 2002, 2003, 2004): Tallinn, Central Bank of Estonia, *www.eestipank.info*
Quarterly Bulletin of Balance of Payments of the Republic of Lithuania (2000, 2001, 2002, 2003, 2004): Riga, Central Bank of Latvia, *www.bank.lv*
Quarterly Bulletin of Balance of Payments of the Republic of Lithuania (2000, 2001, 2002, 2003, 2004): Vilnius, Bank of Lithuania.
Statistical Yearbooks (2001, 2002, 2003): Riga, Statistical Office of Latvia.
Zashev, P. (2004): *Russian Investments in Lithuania-Politics, Business, Corporate Culture*, Electronic publication of Pan-European Institute, 10, *www.tukkk.fi/pei/pub.*
Vahtra, P. and K. Liuhto (2004): *Expansion or Exodus?–Foreign Operations of Russia's Largest Corporations.* Electronic Publication of Pan-European Institute, No. 8, *www.tukkk.fi/pei/pub.*
Vahtra, P. and H. Lorentz (2004): Russian Involvement in Finnish Companies–the Energy Sector in Focus, Electronic Publication of Pan-European Institute, No. 11, *www.tukkk.fi/pei/pub.*
World Investment Report (2004): The Shift Towards Services, Geneva and New York, United Nations.
World Investment Directory (2003): Volume VIII, Central and Eastern Europe 2003, Geneva and New York, United Nations.

products is carried out by the Birzai Pump Station through pipelines, and oil exports and imports are being undertaken through the Butinge Terminal (Figure 2).

The current estimate suggests that the projected capacity of the refinery will reach 15 million tons per annum. In order to use its capacity to an optimal level, MN does not process only crude oil but also various kinds of staple as well. Hence, gas condensate, boiler oil, medium distillates are produced too. The company's production generally meets the European standards and MN has been successfully exporting to Latvia, Poland and West European countries (http://www.nafta.lt).

Currently, the following pipelines are located in Lithuania: crude oil pipeline Pollock-Birzai-Ventspils, Pollock-Birzai-Mazeikiai and processed oil pipeline Iluste-Birzai-Ventspils. A pipeline to the Butinge Terminal has been built during the Lithuanian independence from Russia seeking to diminish MN's dependence on Russian oil supply whilst maximizing the possibility of exporting oil products.

FIGURE 2. The Main Activities of Mazeikiu Nafta

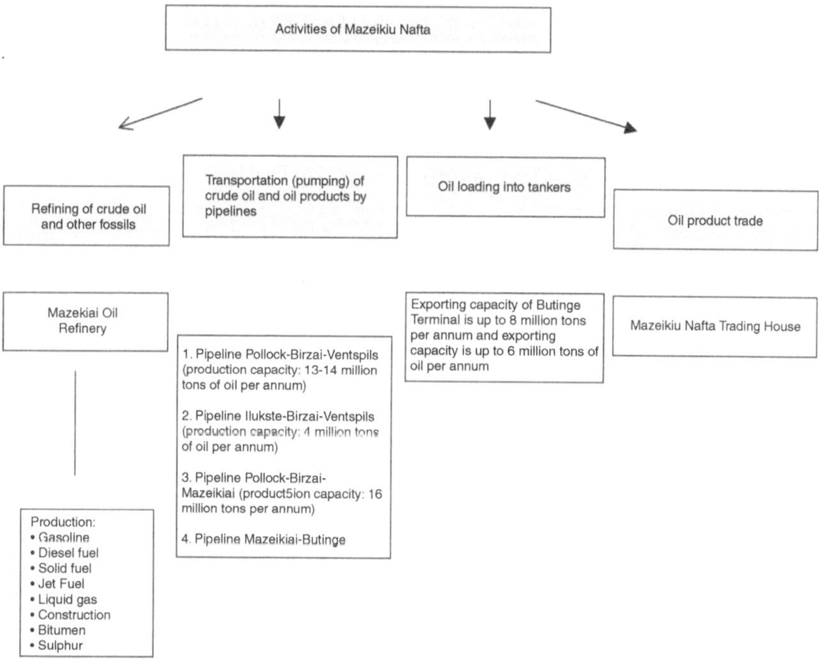

To illustrate the vulnerability of oil transporting activity, it is sufficient to glance at the following figures: in 1995 18 million tons of oil was transported, in 1999 24 million tons, and in 2001 volume of oil being transported reached 30 million tons. During 2002 and 2004, transportation activity diminished by a third to 20 million tons per year. This in large measure has to do with the political development.

THE COMPANY HISTORY OF MAZEIKIU NAFTA

Mazekiu Nafta has evolved gradually. In 1966, oil transporting construction started, which included the Birzai Pump Station as part of oil transporting arterial Pollock-Ventspils. In 1970, the Birzai Pump Station started its performance. In 1979, the oil transport system Pollock-Birzai-Mazeikiai was finished, and a year later, the first production of boiler oil commenced. Hence in 1980, MN oil refinery started its operations with the processing capacity of 12 million tons per annum (http://www.nafta.lt).

In 1990, Lithuania separated from the Soviet Druzhba system. It separated its oil transportation, refining and established two public companies: Naftotiekis and Mazeikiu Nafta. In 1992, MN's oil refining was reduced to 4 million tons compared to 13 million tons in 1989. It meant a major economic shock for Mazeikiu Nafta. To detail the drop in oil supply we need to recall Russia's economic blockade, which started in 1990, when Lithuania declared its independence. Then, refining of oil stopped for a while and after some time the supply was renewed in minor quantities (Figure 3).

The economic shock caused by Russia was multiplied by the shortsightedness and neglect of the Lithuanian authorities. In other words, in 1992-1993 the Lithuanian Government set fixed prices on oil products, while crude oil prices in Russia at the same time skyrocketed; that is to say that it increased from 527 rubles to 47,000 rubles per ton.

In 1993, as a delayed reaction to an already extremely complicated position, the idea of constructing the Butinge Terminal was gaining currency. The decision was made in an attempt to obtain possibility of exporting and importing oil from alternative sources. The absence of crude oil in the country affected not only the MN oil refinery but oil transportation business as well. The Birzai Pump Station suffered in terms of an underutilization of its production capacity. As a result, it was unable to reach its projected revenue. The Butinge Terminal whilst under construction did not manage to attract additional capital.

FIGURE 3. Oil Refining Volume (Million Tons) and the Production Capacity Usage (Percent) in 1989-2003

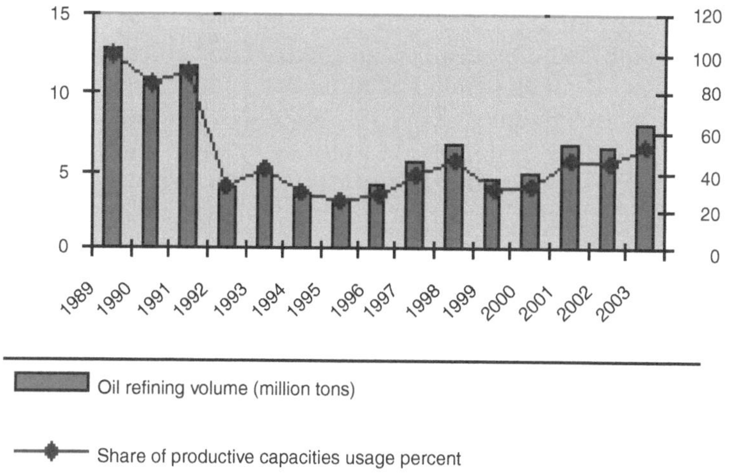

Therefore, in 1998 it was decided to combine the state-owned shares of the Mazekiu Nafta oil refinery, the Birzai Pump Station and the Butinge Terminal in an attempt to form one oil group. It was believed that such a structural reorganization would facilitate inflows of foreign capital via the privatization of a certain part of the group.

In October 1999, after protracted political negotiations, a third of the Mazeikiu Nafta group was purchased by an American company, namely Williams International. The privatization was made through the following procedure: at the very end of 1998, shareholders decided to increase authorized capital by 33%. This enabled Williams International to buy into the company, but at the same time, it managed to gain outright control over MN as well.

Even if the privatization is often seen as the explanation to increased efficiency (Bortolotti & Siniscalco, 2004; Megginson et al., 1994), it was not the case in MN. Williams International neither was able to insure crude oil provision nor eager to modernize the company in order to increase operation efficiency. Some refining accomplishment processes were started in 1999 but it slowed down due to a lack of finance (http://www.nafta.lt).

The Russian oil company, Lukoil, agreed to provide up to 6 million tons of oil per year for a market-based price. However, Lukoil was not interested in supplying oil for the Lithuanian refinery. Its interests were focused on the expansion of its oil product markets.

In 2000, Lukoil and Mazeikiu Nafta started negotiations in order to form a strategic alliance embracing crude oil supply and oil products realization in the Baltic States, Poland and the CIS. The negotiations with Lukoil did not exclude parallel negotiations with another Russian company, Yukos. In September 2000, Mazeikiu Nafta signed an agreement with Yukos for provision of 14 million tons of crude oil per year through the Butinge Terminal. Nevertheless, the process of supply was quite complicated as Yukos, similar to Lukoil, was interested in acquiring a stake in MN.

The agreement between MN and Yukos did not stop Lukoil. The two Russian oil companies competed actively. Lukoil purchased 33% of MN shares. Nevertheless, the economic war was won by Yukos, which unexpectedly managed to sign a contract with the American company Williams, as it purchased 27% of MN for USD 75 million and made a further commitment to invest a corresponding sum into Mazeikiu Nafta. Additionally, Yukos took on the responsibility of providing 5 million tons through pipelines and 4 million tons via the Butinge Terminal for 10 years.

MN's authorized capital had to be diminished and two new share emissions had to be bought by Yukos. Finally, MN's authorized capital has been diminished twice up to 517 million Lithuanian litas and two new share emissions–58 million and 132 million–have been acquired by Yukos. After the transaction, Williams and Yukos had a 27% stake whilst 41% of the share still belonged to the state.

Yukos, similar to Williams earlier, provided Mazeikiu Nafta long-term credit worth USD 75 million with a 10% interest. In August 2002, Williams decided to refinance its credit to MN. Rumors about insolvency of Williams spread out. Sooner after, its 27% stake and management rights were purchased by Yukos for USD 85 million. Yukos refinanced Williams' credit to MN as well. The final distribution of stake was as follows: 54% of the shares belonged to Yukos and 41% was owned by the Lithuanian Government.

In 2003, Mazeikiu Nafta established Mazeikiu Nafta trading company, which specialized in oil product trade. Yukos completed the first stage of planned modernization, which was necessary to meet the quality requirements set for oil products being exported to the EU (see Figure 4).

In 2003, the Russian company continued to improve MN's financial performance. It reached a profit of 208 million litas, equaling USD 76 million, by mainly ensuring supply of raw material (Damauskas, 2004).

FIGURE 4. MN Turnover and Financial Results from 1993 to 2003

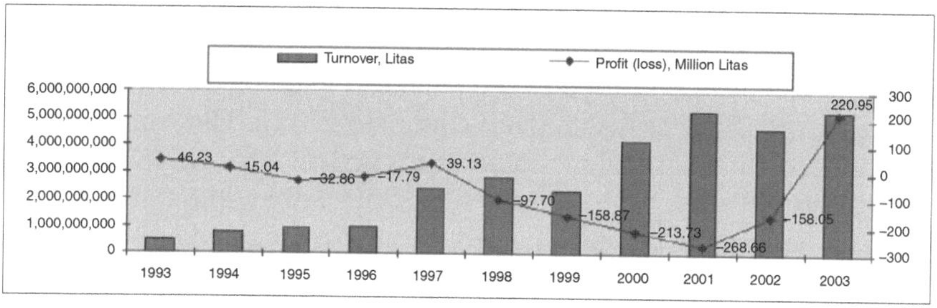

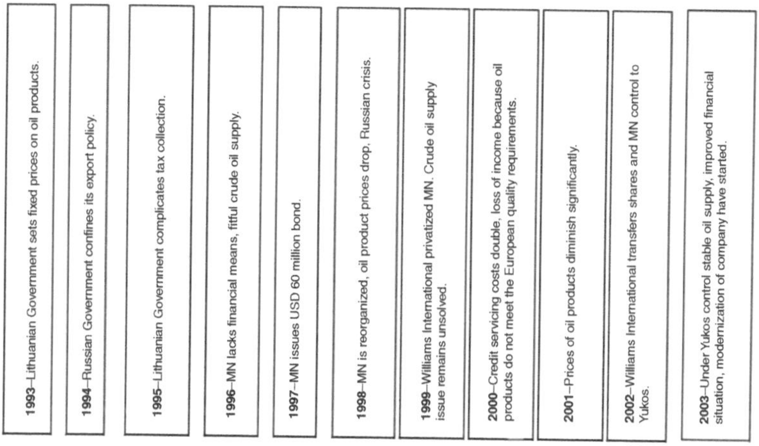

In addition to improved supply which contributed to a better financial outcome, the management costs were reduced. Under Williams, the management and administrative costs of MN grew constantly, whereas under Yukos, management costs reduced from 48 million in 2002 to 29 million litas in 2003. An increase in management efficiency contributed to an improvement of MN financial results. In January 2005, MN's share price increased by almost 10% (Dubauskas, 2005).

CONCLUSIONS

Mazeikiu Nafta, an oil company established in the Soviet era, has been an integral part of the Russian oil transportation and production system. After Lithuania regained its independence, the situation became extremely complicated for the company.

The Lithuanian Government attempted to rely on an American company, which was later found to be unable to guarantee sufficient supply of crude oil. This has resulted in a complete failure. The American company used the Lithuanian situation exclusively for its own financial purposes. All attempts to operate Mazeikiu Nafta without the participation of the Russian capital have led to major financial devastation of the company.

Mazeikiu Nafta vividly illustrates the complexity of the economic separation from integral Russian oil supply-production-sales system. The oil giant found itself in a position where it owns production capacity, but lacks raw materials. A lack of access to oil resources finally conditioned the return of Russian economic dictate over the independence of Lithuania.

REFERENCES

AB Mažeikių nafta 2000 metų prospektas–ataskaita. http://www.lsc.lt

AB Mažeikių nafta akcijų emisijos memorandumas. 1995 06 24 Santarvė, Mažeikių valstybinės įmonės "Nafta" direktorių valdybos narių pareiškimas visuomenei, valdžios institucijoms.

AB Mažeikių nafta obligacijų emisijos memorandumas. Vilnius, 1997.

AB Mažeikių nafta ûkinės–finansinės veiklos analizė 1998 m.,1999 m. http://www.jt.lt

Bernardo Bortolotti, Domenico Siniscalco. The Problem of Privatization: An International Analysis. New York: Oxford University Press, 2004, 200 pp.

Damauskas, Ž. Mažeikių nafta–vėl dėmesio centre. Lietuvos rytas, 2004 m. sausio 27 d. 1995 04 08 Santarvė//Iš įmonės metraščio. Kaip buvo kuriamas naftos gigantas.

Danilevičiūtės, V. Naftininkai ieško paramos. Respublika. 1995 01 19.

Hervé Alexandre and Gerard Charreaux. Efficiency of French privatizations: A dynamic vision. Université de Bourgogne, Iae, Pôle d'économie et de gestion 2, Boulevard Gabriel, BP 26611, 21066, Dijon Cedex, France.

http://www.nafta.lt

Kiesus, G. Pagrindinės mūsų problemos. Fakelas. AB "Mažeikių nafta" savaitraštis. 1996 03 15.

Megginson, W.L., Nash, R.C. and Van Randenborgh, M., 1994. The financial and operating performance of newly privatized firms: An international empirical analysis. Journal of Finance 59, pp. 403-452.

Norma Martínez Laguna. Oil policies and privatization strategies in Mexico: Implications for the petrochemical sector and its production spaces. Institute of Geography, National University of Mexico (UNAM), Circuito Exterior, Ciudad Universitaria, Delegación.

Sytas, A. Skolindami "Mažeikių naftai" Lietuvos bankai įrodo brandumą. Verslo žinios, 2002, Nr. 131 (6 psl.).
Vilniaus bankas. Lietuvos naftos pramonė.
Vyriausybės 1995 04 25 nutarimas 585 "Dėl mokesčių už naftos produktus, pagamintus AB Mažeikių nafta," surinkimo tvarkos.

Russian Direct Investments in Poland: A Case of Lukoil

Małgorzata Runiewicz

SUMMARY. The article describes the expansion of the Russian direct investments in Poland, especially in the oil sector, illustrated with an example of Lukoil. Apart from the capital transfer, the company contributed to long-term sustainable economic development by implementing environmentally friendly production technologies. However, corruption and political involvement related to the expansion of the Russian investments in the strategic assets had negative impact on the perception of Russian investments in Poland. *[Article copies available for a fee from The Haworth Document Delivery Service: 1-800-HAWORTH. E-mail address: <docdelivery@haworthpress.com> Website: <http://www.HaworthPress.com> © 2005 by The Haworth Press, Inc. All rights reserved.]*

KEYWORDS. Russian investments in Poland, Lukoil

INTRODUCTION

The inflow of foreign direct investments (FDI) to Poland has been growing dramatically during the past 10 years. The overall inward FDI

Małgorzata Runiewicz is Assistant Professor, Transformation, Integration, Globalization Economic Research Institute (TIGER), Kozminski Academy of Entrepreneurship and Management, Jagiellonska Street 59, Warsaw 01-103, Poland (E-mail: mruniewi@tiger.edu.pl).

[Haworth co-indexing entry note]: "Russian Direct Investments in Poland: A Case of Lukoil." Runiewicz, Małgorzata. Co-published simultaneously in *Journal of East-West Business* (The Haworth Press, Inc.) Vol. 11, No. 3/4, 2005, pp. 85-95; and: *Expansion or Exodus: Why Do Russian Corporations Invest Abroad?* (ed: Kari Liuhto) The Haworth Press, Inc., 2005, pp. 85-95. Single or multiple copies of this article are available for a fee from The Haworth Document Delivery Service [1-800-HAWORTH, 9:00 a.m. - 5:00 p.m. (EST). E-mail address: docdelivery@haworthpress.com].

Available online at http://www.haworthpress.com/web/JEB

doi:10.1300/J097v11n03_07

stock in Poland has expanded from three billion US dollars in 1992 to 62 billion in 2002.[1]

Foreign investments carried out in Poland originate mostly from Europe. The majority of the foreign capital came from the Netherlands. The second and third most important groups of foreign investors are German and Austrian companies.[2] Russian direct investments to Poland have been increasing considerably since 1994, due to good investment climate, economic stabilization and significant improvement of the Polish-Russian investment ties. In August 1993, the two governments of Poland and Russia signed the *'Agreement on the Construction of a Gas Pipeline System for the Transit of Russian Gas Through the Territory of the Republic of Poland and Supplies of Russian Gas to the Republic of Poland.'* The total value of the Russian direct investment in Poland has reached USD 1,292 million, which gave the Russian Federation the 10th position in 2003.

Most of the German and Dutch companies have invested into high- and medium-high industries (such as the automobile industry and engineering). Correspondingly, French companies have invested in medium-high and medium-low industries (such as food, beverages and services), whereas Russian investments have gone to low-tech and resource-based industries (such as the energy sector or food and confectionary products).

The article deals with a Russian oil company, Lukoil, in Poland. The company is one of the world's biggest oil companies, and therefore, it is particularly interesting to analyze the company's entry strategy to the Polish market. The reminder of the article proceeds as follows. Section 2 makes an overview on the Russian direct investments in Poland. Section 3 deals with Lukoil's activities in Poland. The article ends with concluding remarks.

THE RUSSIAN DIRECT INVESTMENTS IN POLAND

The Russian direct investment abroad has been substantially increasing from the beginning of transition process in the early 1990s. Russian direct investment abroad has flown to a large extent to Central Eastern European countries and to the former Soviet republics. The oil and natural gas businesses form the lion's share of the Russian investments abroad.

According to Poland's statistics, some USD 1.3 billion of Russian capital has been placed in Poland. Russia is the 10th largest investor in

Poland with her 2% stake. The three biggest Russian companies in Poland are Gazprom, Lukoil and Bagdasarian.

Gazprom has equity investments at least in two Polish companies: Gas Trading and Europol Gaz. The overwhelming majority of Gazprom's investments in Poland have been placed in Europol Gaz. Gazprom holds a 48% stake of Europol Gaz. This company owns the gas pipeline, Yamal-Europe, inside the Polish territory.[3]

Lukoil, the second biggest Russian investor in Poland, has invested USD 5.5 million to wholesale of fuels and fuel station network. Lukoil's total foreign assets are worth some USD six billion, which shows the small significance of the investment in Poland in comparison to the company's worldwide activities. Nearly a fifth of the corporation's reserves are located abroad, with major shares in Iraq, the Azeri, Egypt and Kazakh sectors of the Caspian Sea.[4]

The third biggest Russian enterprise in Poland–Bagdasarian–has invested into manufacture of food products, beverages and tobacco. The company has invested USD 2.6 million into the Polish confectionery company Śnieżka S.A. in Świebodzice.

According to the statistical authorities of Poland, in 2003 there were some 177 companies in Poland, where the Russian investment is below one million US dollars. The number seems to be rather stable since 1998 compared to 138 of such companies in 1994. The majority of these companies operate in low-tech/resource-based industries and to a lesser extent services, such as financial, trade, intermediation and consulting. Here are some examples of the Russian owned-companies in Poland: Sungo (wood processing), Multiko (food manufacturing), Polsko-Rosyjska Spółka Węglowa, Gas-Trading, (production of petroleum and coal), Intrall and Elharmes (manufacture of machinery except electrical), Medpol (production of medical equipment), Euromed (professional scientific, measuring and control equipment) and Taloka (financial intermediation).

The majority of the Russian-owned companies was involved in foreign trade. Following the statistical report of 2003, an overall export volume of these companies amounted to USD 600 million (2.7% of the country's total exports), whereas imports totaled almost USD 2500 million (7.7% of the country's total imports).

The regional distribution of the Russian-owned firms indicates that most of them are located in the cities of the North and Southeast Poland (e.g., Lublin, Bialystok and Warsaw).

A CASE STUDY OF A RUSSIAN OIL COMPANY IN POLAND: LUKOIL

History of Lukoil

In November 1991, three oil-producing enterprises, Langepasneftegaz, Uraineftegaz and Kogalymneftegaz, and three processing enterprises, Permorgsintez, the Volgograd and Novoufimsk Refineries, united in an open joint stock company, Lukoil. In 1993, the company's charter capital was entrusted with controlling interests of nine oil-producing, distribution and service companies of Western Siberia, Urals and the Volga region. American Atlantic Richfield Company (ARCO) became a major shareholder and a strategic partner of Lukoil. It became the first Russian company that obtained a full secondary listing on the London Stock Exchange.

In 2000, a new oil field was discovered at the Severny block of the Northern Caspian. In 2002, the Lukoil management published a program of the company restructuring for the period till 2010. The main objectives of the program were to increase profitability and shareholder value of Lukoil.[5] In the same year the company started construction of an oil terminal on the island of Vysotsky, the Leningrad Oblast (close to Finland's border).

In 2003, the company signed general agreement on strategic partnership with Gazprom for the period of 2002-2005. The agreement provided for developing mutually beneficial cooperation in the area of oil and gas exploration, production, transporting and processing, as well marketing of oil and gas, oil and gas products, chemicals and petrochemicals. It also deals with electrical and thermal energy generating and marketing.

Summing up the company's business performance: the consolidated reserves of the company has reached 19.7 billion barrels of oil, thus becoming second among the world oil companies in terms of reserves.

In 2003, oil production the company totaled 81.5 million tons (including production of all subsidiaries and associates), of which 78.6 million tons is in Russia. Average production rose by nearly 50% from 24.4 tons per day in 2002 to 35.7 tons per day in 2003. The company is practically in the hands of Russian owners (96%), with 194 Russian and 20 foreign shareholders.

Measured by foreign assets, Lukoil clearly ranks as the number one oil company in Russia. In terms of reserves and production, Lukoil ranks among the leading oil majors in the world. Although Lukoil maintained the leading position in the sector, its production growth lags behind of that of its main rivals, Yukos and TNK-BP; the former already overtook Lukoil in production terms during the last months of 2003.[6] In worldwide comparison of private oil companies, Lukoil ranks sixth in terms of production and second in proven oil reserves.[7] In 2004, the profits of Shell reached about USD 17.5 billion, whereas Lukoil's net profit amounted to some USD 4 billion.

Lukoil's Activities Abroad

Lukoil is represented in over 30 countries. The company is the largest non-financial transnational corporations based in Central and Eastern Europe. Lukoil's sales network covers 17 countries, including Russia, the CIS (Azerbaijan, Belarus, Georgia, Moldova, Ukraine), Europe (Bulgaria, Hungary, Cyprus, Latvia, Lithuania, Poland, Serbia, Romania, Czech Republic, Estonia) and the USA.

The company's foreign operations include upstream, refining, and marketing activities. The sales of petroleum products through the retail network in 2003 were six million tons, of which 2.4 million tons were sold in Russia, 1.2 in Europe, and 2.4 in the USA. The company's major foreign fields are located in Iraq, the Azeri and Kazakh sectors of the Caspian Sea, and Egypt. Three quarters of the company's proven foreign reserves lie in the Iraqi's West Qurna field, estimated to be one of the largest in the world with the potential reserves of some 20 billion barrrels.[8]

In 2004, Lukoil won a tender for a major gas block in Saudi Arabia, granting the company an 80% stake in a joint venture with Saudi Aramco. In 2003, Lukoil acquired a 25% stake in Anaran oil block in Iran, potentially holding up to 2.5 billion barrels of crude. In 1996, a joint venture was formed between Lukoil and the Italian company, Agip, to carry out foreign exploration and development projects in Egypt and Azerbaijan. Furthermore, Lukoil plans to raise its foreign oil and gas output from its current 4% to some 10-15% of total by 2013 in the Middle East.[9]

Lukoil has also acquired controlling stakes in three foreign refineries in Central East Europe: Bulgaria, Romania, and Ukraine. The company has signed an agreement with the Ukrainian Naftogaz Ukrainy to establish a joint venture for motor oil and lubricant manufacturing. In 2002, these foreign refineries made some 17% of Lukoil's refining activities .

Altogether Lukoil has an extensive retail network of over 4,700 stations, nearly 900 of which are located in other former Soviet republics and Eastern Europe. Lukoil has also gained a foothold in the USA, where the company owns a network of retail stations. In 2000, along with the takeover of a US company, Getty Petroleum Marketing (GPM), Lukoil acquired some 1,300 filling stations in the USA.[10] In July 2001, Lukoil acquired a Canadian company, Bitech Petroleum, operating in Colombia, Egypt and Tunisia. Even if Lukoil has considerable stakes in oil fields abroad, foreign production accounted for only some 4% of the group's total oil and gas condensate production in 2002.[11]

Lukoil in Poland

Lukoil applied a traditional entry strategy in Poland.[12] The company established in 1997 a limited liability company under the name Lukoil Poland, where all the shares are owned by the Lukoil Group. There are two major fields of Lukoil's economic activity in Poland. Lukoil Poland specializes in both wholesale and retail sales of the Russian liquid petroleum gas as well as in the distribution of the oil lubricants. The above mentioned liquid petroleum gas is based on propane-butane elements and is abbreviated as LPG.

At present, propane-butane and natural gas are the most commonly used gaseous fuels in transportation. Natural gas is used mostly in compressed (CNG) and to some extent also in liquefied forms (LNG–Liquefied Natural Gas). LNG fuel stations are very similar to fuel stations that sell LPG. The difference is that gas is transported and stored in cryogenic tanks under very low temperatures of −160 to −170°C, which is reflected by the technology used.

Since 1997, Lukoil had been gradually expanding the scope of its activities on the Polish market. In 2002, Lukoil Poland's turnover reached USD 35 million. According to the company's forecast this number has significantly increased in 2004. Lukoil Poland is the leading supplier of the LPG to the Polish market.

Lukoil's sales and distribution activity in Poland is represented by the Polish-owned company ADWA Group, which has long-term experience (operated in the Polish market since 1986) in the regional trade networks activity. The company has a well-developed logistics system, including storage facilities and transport equipment.

Since its establishment, ADWA has become one of the leading distributors on the Polish oil market. Starting from 2001, ADWA became the single distributor of the Gdansk Refinery products in 26 Polish districts. In 2002, the company has received the quality certificate ISO 9002.[13]

Despite an uncertain economic and political situation in the company as well as worsening climate for the Russian investments in Poland, Lukoil decided to make other steps towards a full and direct entry to the Polish market.

In April 2003, Lukoil teamed up with London-based partner Rotch Energy to bid one billion US dollars for the state-owned Gdansk Refinery.[14] However, due to the nationalistic elements of the Polish press and political elite the agreement has not been signed.[15] The refinery remains unsold. Despite the unsuccessful attempt, Lukoil is still interested in the refinery, and hence it prepares a new bid.

In addition to the Gdansk Refinery, Lukoil also has other strategic interests in the Polish market. One of them is the participation in the privatization of Lotos Group and a possible contract with Pern i Naftoport. Both companies specialize in the oil transport to Western Europe. Neither of the transactions have been signed so far.

There are several reasons for Lukoil's failures. For instance, Poland's dominant fuel company PKN Orlen objected to Lukoil's expansion to Poland. PKN Orlen, supplying 60% of Poland's gasoline market, faced pressure on narrowing its profit margins with the entrance of a major player such as Lukoil.[16]

There are arguments both against and in favor of Lukoil's business activity in the Polish energy market. Arguments against Lukoil's expansion focus on the political interest of Russia in Poland. Arguments in favor of Lukoil's relate to possible economic gains, which result from Lukoil's contribution to the energy infrastructure development. Furthermore, allowing PKN Orlen to gain control of the Gdansk Refinery would give it a control of more than 75% of the Polish gasoline market. Such monopolistic power could be harmful to the independent fuel station owners and is inconsistent with the EU competition legislation. Moreover, such monopolistic power would make the gas and oil prices less advantageous for the consumers.

Summa summarum, it can be stated that the role of Lukoil in the Polish energy market is marginal. Consequently, it can be argued that the significance of Lukoil Poland in the overall capital of the Lukoil Group is very limited. Even if Lukoil's investment in Poland plays a marginal role in the whole group's investment decisions, Poland remains an important subject of the company's outward expansion.

Lukoil's Next Steps in Poland

Lukoil puts high priority on protection of the environment and natural resources management. As a result of this policy, Lukoil Poland has focused on the production of liquid gas, which produces so called 'universal' energy. In comparison to other sources of energy, it has more competitive prices and lower exploitation costs. But mostly liquid gas is a modern ecological source of energy and does not create any danger to the environment in its production, process and utilization, and that means it is less toxic.

Lukoil has built a modern liquid gas plant in Bydgoszcz, and a highly-reputed network of 130 automatic gas stations (110 is own by Lukoil Poland). The company has 70,000 gas bottles, which can be inter-exchanged in 1,600 distribution centers and professional transport equipment.

Lukoil Poland's investment program for the year 2004 is some USD 10 million. The company's main mission is to develop further the sales and distribution of Lukoil's products in Poland. The investment program focuses on the construction and new network of gas stations. The company wants to increase sales turnovers in LPG and gain 15% of the Polish market. Moreover, the Lukoil management expects to establish two more gas filling stations of LPG, a loading terminal, oil tanks and additional sales centers of gas in bottles and containers.

Lukoil Poland plans to start delivering petrochemical products to the Polish market from the Lukoil's plants located in Kalush (Ukraine) and Budionovsk (Russia). Since the year 2004, the company has been offering its own ready made petroleum products under the trademark of Lukoil. It was possible due to the capital involvement and co-operation with independent market actors.

Despite the unsuccessful attempt to gain the investment share in the privatization of the Gdansk Refinery, Lukoil plans to build at least 50 new stations in Poland, which will fully adjust the quality standards of the European Union.

CONCLUSION

Poland is one of the largest FDI host countries in CEE. Poland has a considerable absorption capacity for petroleum and gas products. Like Bulgaria or Ukraine, Poland should be a natural market for Russia's biggest companies, especially for its oil producers, such as Lukoil.

However, Poland's position as a location for operations of the Russian companies has not evolved much. The share of Russian oil in the Polish energy market is marginal. Due to Lukoil's relatively small investments in Poland, Lukoil's impact on the Polish economy is rather limited. Here, we should, however, differentiate the direct and the indirect impact of Lukoil's business expansion on Poland's economy.

The direct impact on the energy sector and the whole economy can be regarded as rather positive. This article reveals that apart from the capital transfer the company contributed to long-term sustainable economic development by implementing environmentally friendly production technologies. To a limited extent, the company has also stimulated the Polish exports of petroleum products and decreased the growing deficit in the Polish current account in the relations with Russia (Poland has the largest trade deficit with Russia). Other positive developments include guarantees for long-term supplies of unprocessed fuels from Russia. It is also important to underline that Lukoil has a very clear investment development plan for Poland.

The indirect negative impact of the Lukoil investment in Poland results from the corruption and political involvement related to the expansion of the Russian investments in the strategic assets (e.g., Lukoil's participation in the privatization of the Gdansk Refinery). The memories of the Soviet domination often cause offensive reactions towards the Russian companies in Poland and in other former socialist countries. The history explains why Poland and other countries of the region favor western investment over Russian ones.

The EU enlargement opens new business opportunities for the Russian companies and their investments in the energy sector. It is expected that, Russia's aim to become a member of the World Trade Organization will increase its credibility as a business partner and contribute to an increase of the Russian direct investments in the region.[17]

NOTES

1. The Polish Agency for Foreign Investment, http://www.paiz.gov.pl.
2. http://www.paiz.gov.pl.
3. Liuhto and Jumpponen, *The Internationalization Boom of Russian Corporations–Studies of Russian Banks, Energy and Metal Companies*, Research Report No. 135, 2002, Lappeenranta University of Technology.
4. Vahtra and Liuhto, *Expansion or exodus–foreign operations of the Russia's largest corporations,* Electronic Publications of Pan-European Institute, 8/2004, http://www.tukkk.fi/pei/pub.

5. In the short term the accomplishment of these objectives would be promoted by the growth of export operations, higher revenues, optimization of the well stock, cost reduction, improved production efficiency and reorganization of the company's structure (http://www.lukoil.com.pl).

6. Vahtra and Liuhto, *Expansion or exodus . . .* op. cit.

7. Ibidem.

8. Ibidem.

9. Recent removal of the sanctions on Iraq have initiated promising negotiations between Iraqi and Russian representatives, to restart the operations on the field, but significant exploration operations are unlikely to start before considerable security improvements in the region (Ibidem).

10. This retail network was extended by the acquisition of 795 stations from ConocoPhillips in 2004 for the price of $266 million (Vahtra & Liuhto, *Expansion or exodus . . .* op. cit.).

11. Ibidem.

12. Bulatov, *Russian Direct Investment Abroad: Main Motivations in the Post-Soviet Period.* Transnational Corporations 7, UNCTAD, New York 1998.

13. http://www.adwa.com.pl.

14. The Gdansk Refinery's network includes 300 gasoline stations, serving 17% of the Polish market.

15. Political fears, however, do not find support in the public opinion. According to the daily Polish *Rzeczpospolita* published poll report some 51% of the public viewed investments by big Russian companies as not in the national interest (http://www.rzeczpospolita.pl).

16. http://www.wnp.pl/np.

17. Runiewicz, M., "Russian Direct Investments in the Transport and Energy Infrastructure of the Baltic States and Their Impact on the Export Competitiveness of Estonia, Latvia and Lithuania on EU Markets in 1992-2002," in *A Wider Europe and The New Neighbourhood Policy of The European Union*, Warsaw School of Economics, Warsaw 2004, pp. 96-97.

REFERENCES

Bank of Finland. 2001. Russian Economy: The Month in Review. Institute for Economies in Transition, Helsinki: Bank of Finland 5.

Bulatov, A., Russian Direct Investment Abroad: Main Motivations in the Post-Soviet Period. *Transnational Corporations* 7, UNCTAD, New York, 1998.

Business Central Europe. 2001. July/August 8: 14.

European Bank for Reconstruction and Development. *Russian Federation Investment Profile in 2001*, EBRD, London, 2001.

Hill, M., "Soviet and Eastern European Company Activity in the United Kingdom and Ireland," in G. Hamilton ed., *Red Multinationals or Red Herrings?–The Activities of Enterprises from Socialist Countries in the West.* London: Pinter, 1986.

Hunya G. & Stankowsky, J., Foreign Direct Investment in Central and East European Countries and the Former Soviet Union, *WIIW-WIFO Database*, June, 2001.

Liuhto, K. & Jumpponen, J., *The Internationalization Boom of Russian Corporations–Studies of Russian Banks, Energy and Metal Companies*, Research Report No. 135, 2002, Lappeenranta University of Technology.

Runiewicz, M., "Russian Direct Investments in the Transport and Energy Infrastructure of the Baltic States and Their Impact on the Export Competitiveness of Estonia, Latvia and Lithuania on EU Markets in 1992-2002," in *A Wider Europe and The New Neighbourhood Policy of The European Union*, Warsaw School of Economics, Warsaw, 2004.

Vahtra, P. & Liuhto, K., *Expansion or exodus–foreign operations of Russia's largest corporations*, Electronic Publications of Pan-European Institute, 8/2004, http://www.tukkk.fi/pei/pub.

Zorska, A., *Transnational Corporations in Poland*, Leon Koźmiński Academy of Entrepreneurship and Management, Warsaw, 2003.

Websites:

ADWA group–http://www.adwa.com.pl.
The Europol Gaz Company website–http://www.europolgaz.com.pl.
http://www.compiler.fi.
Lukoil Poland–http://www.lukoil.com.pl.
Pan-European Institute–http://www.tukkk.fi/pei/e.
Polish Agency for Foreign Investment–http://www.paiz.gov.pl.
Red Square Ltd.–http://www.redsq.ipl.net.
Wirtualny Nowy Przemysl–http://www.wnp.pl/np.

Yukos' Stake in Slovak Transpetrol

Viera Pochybova

SUMMARY. In 2002, Yukos was the ideal investor for Slovak Transpetrol, as Yukos was one of the Russia's largest oil producers, and hence had enough oil to fill Transpetrol's pipelines. Just as important, Yukos was the standard-bearer for Russia's more transparent, well-managed oil sector. Unlike some Russian energy companies, Yukos' conduct never raised suspicions that it was acting as an agent for the Russian State in its former empire. Nevertheless, the situation at the beginning of 2005 is different from 2002. Yukos' forthcoming bankruptcy negates all those advantages because of which Yukos was welcomed as the strategic investor and leaves the Slovak Government with a lot of additional problems. For any decision that the Slovak Government would like to undertake, the agreement of the Russian side is necessary. No swift resolution is likely. Important decisions about the future of the respective oil industry may be made in Moscow rather than in Bratislava.

KEYWORDS. Russian investments in Slovakia, Transpetrol, Yukos

---

Viera Pochybova was a Visiting Researcher from the Slovak Republic at the Turku School of Economics and Business Administration in 2004.

[Haworth co-indexing entry note]: "Yukos' Stake in Slovak Transpetrol." Pochybova, Viera. Co-published simultaneously in *Journal of East-West Business* (The Haworth Press, Inc.) Vol. 11, No. 3/4, 2005, pp. 97-107; and: *Expansion or Exodus: Why Do Russian Corporations Invest Abroad?* (ed: Kari Liuhto) The Haworth Press, Inc., 2005, pp. 97-107. Single or multiple copies of this article are available for a fee from The Haworth Document Delivery Service [1-800-HAWORTH, 9:00 a.m. - 5:00 p.m. (EST). E-mail address: docdelivery@haworthpress.com].

Available online at http://www.haworthpress.com/web/JEB

doi:10.1300/J097v11n03_08

INTRODUCTION

Russia is a significant trade partner for Slovakia. It is the third most important import partner with 9%.[1] This is mainly due to the imports of energy and minerals (natural gas, oil, coal, and iron ore). The Slovak Republic is a net importer of energy. Slovakia has minor oil resources, and thus is relying on oil imports from Russia to meet approximately 97% of its oil needs. The domestic extraction of oil covers only about 1.5% of domestic consumption.

To meet Slovakia's need of 63,000 barrels per day of oil products, Slovakia imports 90,000 barrels of crude and refined product per day while exporting 29,000 barrels of refined products. To meet the future need for oil, Slovakia recently signed a long-term oil supply contract with Russia through 2008.

Slovakia's major corporation in the oil business, Transpetrol, has the responsibility of administration and operation of the oil pipeline system and storage and distribution of petroleum in Slovakia. Slovnaft is the country's major oil refinery. Petrochema Dubova produces specialty oils and additives, and is a processor of low sulfur petroleum.

Slovakia is a major transit country for Russian natural gas through the Transgas system to other European countries. Since Slovakia's natural gas resources are minor, the country is heavily dependent on imports from Russia.

The role of Russia as foreign investor in Slovakia is subjected to many questions. Russia's share in the Slovak inward FDI stock is less than 1%[2] despite the $74 million investment of Yukos in Slovak Transpetrol and the pre-emption right of Gazprom to buy 16% shares of SPP (Slovak Gas Industry).

The National Bank of Slovakia reports only five companies with Russian capital over 10% and over SKK 1 million, four of them located in Western Slovakia. However, the cooperation with Russia is nowadays being realized through some industrial projects in Slovakia. There is the Slovak-Russian tyre production company Matador-Omskšina. The Russian firms are taking part in the construction of a laser and cyclotron centre. Russian companies are also represented on the market of nuclear power supply. The joint stock company TVEL signed an agreement about nuclear fuel supplies for the nuclear power plants of Jaslovske Bohunice and Mochovce for the years 2005-2010.

This article deals with the development of the Slovak oil pipeline operator Transpetrol after its privatization, when the Russian company Yukos acquired a 49% stake in Traspetrol. In the centre of examination is the impact of Yukos' ownership on Transpetrol and possible future development scenarios in the light of recent events around Yukos.

TRANSPETROL

Transpetrol is the only oil pipeline operator in the Slovak Republic. The geographic position and the relatively high transportation capacity of the Slovak pipeline system create positive conditions for its connection to the European transit routes. The Transpetrol pipeline system is 515 km long, of which 422 km is doubled. It runs the entire length of the Slovak Republic from the Ukrainian border in the east to the Czech Republic in the west, with a branch to a refinery in Bratislava and a connection to the Adria pipeline system running south through Hungary to Croatia. Transpetrol operates five pumping stations and storage facilities along its route, and has approximately 500 employees. Because of its annual turnover, its profit, and number of employees, Transpetrol ranks among Slovakia's most strategic companies.

Transpetrol is a relatively young oil pipeline company. After the change in social-political and economic relations in former Czechoslovakia in 1989, the Czechoslovakian corporation Transpetrol was founded in 1991 to manage the Czechoslovakian section of the Druzhba pipeline system. The split of Czechoslovakia in 1993 and the formation of two separate states caused the stock company to be divided into two individual companies. The stock company MERO ČR was formed in the Czech Republic, whereas the Slovak section retained the original name and the stock company Transpetrol became sole operator of the national oil pipeline system of the Slovak Republic.

Due to the exceptional importance of petroleum transfer and storage for the Slovak economy, Transpetrol was categorized as a strategic enterprise and remained 100% state owned. In 2000, the Slovak Government decided to partially privatize Transpetrol. One of the key factors influencing the decision to privatize was a substantial loss of potential revenue for the state caused by the fact that although the Druzhba pipeline has a projected throughput capacity of nearly 25 million tons per year, it has historically been running at less than half this amount, and experienced a steady decline in throughput in the 1990s. In December 2001, an auction was held for the sale of 49% of the shares in the company to an outside party that would become a strategic partner in the further development of Transpetrol's business. The winner of the auction was the Russian company, Yukos. In the current shareholder structure, the owner of the 51% stake in Transpetrol is the Slovak Republic through the Ministry of Economy; the remaining 49% is owned by Yukos.

The activities of the company include domestic and international transit of oil, as well as storage of oil for commercial customers and State Resource Reserves. Economic results in the oil transportation business in large part depend on actual demand, and consequently on the executed volume of transported oil. Slovakia's largest purchaser of oil is the refinery Slovnaft.

With regard to revenues and utilization of the oil pipeline's capacity, the Czech refineries such as Česká Rafinérska and Paramo play an important role for Transpetrol. This remains to be true despite the fact that oil transport into the Czech Republic has been declining since 1996.

Besides transporting oil, storage plays an important role in Transpetrol's business activities as well. In the last years, Transpetrol has invested SKK 2.5 billion[3] into a construction of storage capacity. The current capacity of oil storage containers reaches 520,000 cubic metres. According to legal regulations and requirements of the European Union, a gradual increase in the volume of stored oil for State Resources Reserves is expected. By 2008, they should cover up to 90 days' consumption of oil and oil products. This level of storage capacity is expected to be reached through further investments into constructing storage containers.

In 2003, Transpetrol transported a total of 10 million tons of crude oil i.e., a growth of 5% compared to 2002. The oil supplies for the only Slovak oil customer, Slovnaft represented 5.5 million tons, which was the highest level reached in the last decade. The increased oil supplies also caused the overall growth of the oil transportation volume for the Czech customers, who play an important role in terms of the use of the capacity of the Slovak oil pipeline system. The decisive proportion of the amount constitutes the supplies for the company, Česká Rafinérska; in 2003 Transpetrol supplied it with 3.6 million tons of oil. In 2003, a pre-tax profit of SKK 450 million was reached, which was 15% above the plan. The transportation revenues in 2003 reached 93% of the turnout on the current activities of the firm reaching SKK 1.6 billion (in 2002 it was SKK 1.5 billion).

THE IMPACT OF THE RUSSIAN GOVERNMENT'S ASSAULT AGAINST YUKOS ON TRANSPETROL

At the end of 2004, it became evident that Yukos had little or no chance of surviving the legal attacks launched against it. Until the end of 2004, it was widely assumed that the company's total tax bill would reach USD 12 billion, a level that would cause considerable damage but did not necessarily imply Yukos's extinction. Even when the authorities made moves to seize Yukos' main production unit, Yuganskneftegaz, there was a chance that Yukos could survive as a smaller oil company. In November 2004, however, the company was given a $9-billion bill for 2002 back taxes plus fines, and the authorities seized Yuganskneftegaz with a view to selling it for a greatly reduced price to partially settle the debt. The auction of Yuganskneftegaz for USD 9.3 billion left Yukos with tax liabilities far greater than its remaining assets, apparently making the company's bankruptcy inevitable.

The authorities' decision to freeze Yukos' bank accounts had already disrupted deliveries to Central East European countries because Yukos was unable to pay the fees required to use the Russian export pipeline system. Hungary and Poland, however, were able to find new Russian oil suppliers. From a supply perspective, the prospective bankruptcy of Yukos promises no more than short-term disruption: oil will continue to be pumped from Yukos' wells, but it will be sold under the name of another operator. For those countries in which Yukos is an investor, however, the outlook is more complicated, which is also the case of Slovak Transpetrol.

Thus, the Yukos affair is beginning to have an unpleasant impact on Slovakia. Worried at the prospect of Yukos' bankruptcy, the Slovak Government is pursuing talks to repurchase the 49% stake in Transpetrol. Moreover, there is justified concern that the bankruptcy of the oil giant could bring negative effects to Slovakia. Yukos does not only own a 49% share of the Slovak pipeline operator, but it is also a significant oil supplier for Slovnaft, and the largest customer of Transpetrol. Thus, the bankruptcy of Yukos would have serious consequences.

The Slovak Ministry of Economy confirmed towards the end of 2004 that it wants to recoup the Transpetrol shares and would do everything possible to regain Yukos' 49% share in the company. This all happened just two and a half years after the Slovak Government sold the shares to Yukos. The Slovak Ministry of Economy wrote a letter to the Russian Government expressing its explicit willingness to negotiate the return of Yukos' shares to Slovakia. The Ministry of Economy acknowledged that the Russian side expressed its interest to an agreement and confirmed that an intensive communication is proceeding.

The stake in the oil transportation company belongs directly to Yukos and it has been arrested along with all of the oil company's other assets and may not be sold without special permission from the

Russian Government. Hence, the fate of the shares will be most probably determined by Russian authorities with little Slovak influence. Since it is probable that the assets of bankrupting Yukos will be gradually sold, the Slovak Government is eager to rescue Transpetrol from Yukos before the Russian firm goes bankrupt, to ensure that no decisions, which have a strategic bearing on the Slovak economy, are taken in another country. The Slovak Government is afraid that when Yukos goes bankrupt, the country will have little influence over who succeeds the Russian company as the operator and 49% owner of Transpetrol.

Unfortunately, the Slovak Government can do little about regaining the stake. Slovakia does not have the option to buy back part or all of the 49% stake in Transpetrol, or to recover from Yukos management control over the enterprise. While Yukos is not pressed to sell the holding, it has reportedly started exploratory talks with the government.

The financial position of the Slovak Government is, however, not that good. Perhaps optimistically, the Ministry of Economy suggested that the price of the 49% stake should be approximately the same as the $74 million that Yukos paid in 2001. It is not clear whether the Russian Government, which must approve any transaction involving Yukos assets, will agree. Slovakia's 2005 budget deficit target is SKK 61.5 billion (USD 2 billion),[4] equal to 3.4% of expected GDP. Although the budget is based on relatively conservative macroeconomic assumptions, the deficit is likely to be swelled by the effects of pension reform, to 3.8% of GDP. At that level, even expenditure of $100 million on Transpetrol would be difficult for the government to justify.

The Slovak Government realizes its financial limitations. The government's preferred option was to buy the stake then hold a tender for its sale. Given the government's limited ability to make the purchase, however, a second option was outlined: to find a new owner in consultation with the Russian Government. The legality of direct selling is, however, questionable. The state's contract with Yukos has a clause prohibiting either party to sell Transpetrol shares to a third entity without the approval of both parties for five years.

It appears unlikely that the Slovak Government will resolve the Yukos-related problems in the short run. On the other hand, Yukos cannot sell its stake without the approval of the Russian Government, which has so far refused all company requests to co-operate in shedding non-core assets in order to reduce the tax debt. This situation seems likely to continue until Yukos is finally pushed into bankruptcy, after which the Russian Government will decide what to do with the Transpetrol stake.

The dilemma that the Slovak Government finds itself in illustrates the risk of dealing with Russia. Yet in common with the neighbors in Central East Europe, it relies on Russian oil supplies and has no realistic alternative. This, added to their determination to make the most of the oil assets bequeathed to it by the Czechoslovakian socialist government, means that Yukos is almost certain to be succeeded as a strategic shareholder in Transpetrol by other Russian companies. The Slovak Government can only hope that it will have some say in the decision and that, next time, they will have an investor able to stay on good terms with the Kremlin.

The Slovak Government's position was made more precarious in early 2005 by the decision of a regional court in Presov (Slovakia) to support the claim of a private business to a 34% stake in Transpetrol. The case dated back to 1995, when a court awarded damages of SKK 40 million ($1.3 million) to businessperson Ignac Ilcisin following a dispute with the tax authority over real estate. At the time, the finance ministry failed to contest the claim and in 1998 an executor offered 34% of the government's shares in Transpetrol as a damage settlement. Those involved–including Mr Ilcisin, the judge and the bailiff–are still under police investigation.

The Presov court ruling is disastrous for the government not only because it threatens to deprive the state of a block of shares worth SKK 2-3 billion. The privatisation deal with Yukos specifically protected the Russian company's shares from any such action, meaning that the 34% to be awarded to Mr Ilcisin would come from the state's 51% shareholding. The Slovak Government would thus lose majority control of Transpetrol, leaving Yukos as the largest single shareholder.

Moreover, the privatisation contract obliges the government to sell 2-3% of Transpetrol to Yukos if the state loses majority control. Unless it can block execution of the regional court decision, and the government appears to have several options to achieve this, the Slovak authorities may thus give up majority control of Transpetrol as well as management rights to Yukos, and thereafter to its creditors.

It remains unclear what fate awaits the Transpetrol joint venture. Slovakia's oil refinery Slovnaft already announced that it is interested in buying the 49% share of the former state-owned oil pipeline operating company Transpetrol. Slovnaft confirmed that if the Slovak Ministry of Economy succeeds in regaining Transpetrol's shares and afterwards offers them for sale, Slovnaft will take part in this privatization. Slovnaft has already expressed its interest to buy the share in Transpetrol.

Co-ownership of Transpetrol would be a tool to secure regular oil supplies to Slovnaft's refineries.

Regarding the two most important companies in the Slovak oil sector, Slovnaft and Transpetrol, it seems that neither of them is as much concerned with the almost certain bankruptcy of Yukos as the Slovak Government is. According to the Transpetrol management, none of the projects of the company is threatened or stopped. For example, construction of a new pipeline between Bratislava and Schwechat refinery is still on the agenda. An Austrian oil company, OMV, claims that on the Austrian side of connection Bratislava-Schwechat, everything is going in accordance with the plan. Both companies, Transpetrol and OMV, are strong enough to carry out the project without Yukos.

The bankruptcy of Yukos could bring two possible scenarios for Transpetrol. Either someone would buy the Russian company or its assets would be sold in bankruptcy procedure. In the case of bankruptcy only the shareholders structure would change–the operation of Transpetrol would remain unchanged. Projects that Yukos realizes in Transpetrol would be attractive also for other owners and thus they are expected to continue. However, some experts point out that if bankruptcy was the case, the change in management system could take place.

Slovnaft claims that the company does not assume any problems concerning oil supplies. Nevertheless, the truth might be different. Slovnaft takes a substantial part of its oil from Yukos from the beginning of the year 2003. Yukos included Slovnaft to oil supplies as a member of the MOL group. This Hungarian syndicate is a long-standing partner of the Russian company. In addition to Yukos, Slovnaft takes oil also from several other Russian companies.

Despite optimistic claims of Slovnaft, in January 2005 Yukos canceled several contracts for oil supplies. The contracts must have been canceled due to the inability of the company to supply the demanded volume after losing its main asset Yuganskneftegaz. This step also affected Slovakia. Hungarian MOL acknowledged that Petroval, Yukos' main business branch, stopped the oil supplies indefinitely. MOL was prepared for such a measure and searched for alternative Russian suppliers to cover the gap caused by supplies cut-off by Yukos. Petroval's measure could affect as much as 60% of oil imports of MOL. The company could replace the insufficiency through oil purchase from other Russian suppliers, such as Lukoil, Sibneft or TNK-BP.

In January 2005, MOL signed a five-year contract with Lukoil for oil supplies in the volume of 5 million tons a year, not only for the mother company in Hungary but also for Slovak Slovnaft. According to the previous 10-year contract, Yukos should have supplied MOL with 7 million tons of oil per year, half for Hungary, and half for Slovakia, which represented more than half of the Slovak oil consumption. Petroval announced that it is enforcing the clause in the oil supplies contracts that enables the company to decrease the supplies in the case of circumstances which are beyond its control. MOL owns majority stake in Slovnaft, which constituted 98% at the end of last year.

CONCLUSION

In 2002, Yukos seemed to be the ideal investor for Slovakia. As one of the Russia's largest producers, it had enough oil to fill Transpetrol's pipelines and thus fully utilize their capacity. The arrival of Yukos was welcomed as the solution to a long-standing oil sector efficiency problem. Transpetrol is an enterprise that requires a high level of crude oil supplies in order to be profitable. In Slovakia, the 515 km section of the east-west Druzhba pipeline was operating at less than half of its annual capacity of 21 million tons.

At the same time, Yukos had the lobbying strength to ensure that the oil was delivered via the Russian state-owned pipeline system. The company was, moreover, a dynamic manager with the financial power and ambition to invest in refinery upgrades, pipeline extensions, and other projects. Just as important, Yukos was the standard-bearer for Russia's more transparent, well-managed oil sector. Unlike some Russian energy companies, Yukos' conduct never raised suspicions that it was acting as an agent for the Russian state in its former empire.

Yukos' arrival had a positive effect on Transpetrol. Crude volumes through the pipeline rose from 9.0 million tons per year in 2000-01 (prior to Yukos' arrival) to 9.5 million tons in 2002 and 9.9 million tons in 2003. Yukos planned to further raise volumes by upgrading a link to the Adria pipeline, which ends at the Croatian deepwater port of Omishalj and had shorter-term plans to increase usage of the pipeline, by constructing a 60 km-extension into Austria to supply crude to the Schwechat refinery, which is owned by OMV (Austria).

Nevertheless, the situation at the beginning of 2005 is different from 2002. Yukos' forthcoming bankruptcy negates all those advantages because of which Yukos was welcomed as the strategic investor and leaves the Slovak Government with a lot of additional problems. Yukos is the direct owner of the 49% stake in Transpetrol, so that shareholding will automatically pass to the company's creditors in the event of bankruptcy.

In the past months, the Slovak Ministry of Economy has stressed the importance of regaining state control over Transpetrol. The government announced its intentions to Yukos in mid-October 2004 and at that time contacted the Russian Government to begin negotiations.

For any decision that the Slovak Government would like to undertake, the agreement of the Russian side is necessary. However, there are two basic possibilities about what could happen to the 49% stake: either the state buys back the respective shares and announces a tender or sells the shares directly to a new interested buyer (with the approval of the Russian Government) without passing the shares on the state.

Anyway, there is one event that can cause that all of the above-mentioned speculations to end up in vain. It is the regional court ruling in Slovakia from the beginning of 2005, which threatens to reduce the state's stake further and trigger an agreement allowing the Russian company to gain majority control, that has made that effort all the more urgent.

Although the most important companies in the Slovak oil industry assure the public that the internal problems of Yukos cannot influence their normal operation, the starting problems with oil supplies and dubious future of Transpetrol indicate a different reality.

To sum it up, Russia's Yukos affair is creating problems for Slovakia. Naturally the country does not wish to be saddled with a bankrupt investor that can no longer supply the oil it needs, but it does not have the right to recover the strategic stakes and management control sold to Yukos, and lacks the financial resources to close a deal quickly. As a result, no swift resolution is likely–and important decisions about the future of the respective oil industry may be made in Moscow rather than in Bratislava.

NOTES

1. www.statistics.sk.
2. Estimation of the author based on the information from www.nbs.sk.
3. www.transpetrol.sk.
4. www.finance.gov.sk.

REFERENCES

ASR (July 2004) Kaspická ropa do Europy cez Druzbu nepotecie. *Pravda*. Available from World Wide Web:(http://tvojepeniaze.pravda.sk).

Balogova, Beata (November 2004). State ogles share. *The Slovak Spectator*. Available from World Wide Web (http://www.slovakspectator.sk).

From press reports (November 2004) Slovnaft wants Transpetrol shares. *The Slovak Spectator*. (http://www.slovakspectator.sk).

Economist Intelligence Unit: www.viewswire.com.

The Economist Intelligence Unit (February 2005). *Eastern Europe economy: Sucked into the Yukos quicksand*. Available from World Wide Web (http://www.viewswire.com).

Embassy of Russian Federation in the Slovak Republic: www.slovakia.mid.ru.

http://www.inogate.org/html/countries/slovakia.htm.

http://www.slovakia.mid.ru/dip-slo.html.

Interstate Oil and Gas Transport to Europe: www.inogate.org.

National Bank of Slovakia: www.nbs.sk.

SITA, Reuters (January 2005) Jukos zrušil niektore ropne kontrakty. *SME*. Available at World Wide Web (http://peniaze.zoznam.sk).

Slovak Daily Newspaper Pravda–online version: www.pravda.sk.

Slovak Daily Newspaper SME: www.sme.sk.

Slovak Ministry of Finance: www.finance.gov.sk.

Slovak Ministry of Economy: www.economy.gov.sk.

Slovak Ministry of Foreign Affairs: www.foreign.gov.sk.

The Slovak Spectator–online version: www.slovakspectator.sk.

Statistical Office of the Slovak Republic: www.statistics.sk.

Transpetrol: www.transpetrol.sk.

Vahtra, Peeter & Liuhto, Kari (August 2004). *Expansion or Exodus? Foreign Operations of Russia's largest Corporations*, Turku School of Economics and Business Administration, Pan-European Institute. Available from World Wide web (http://www.tukkk.fi/pei/pub).

Yukos: www.yukos.com.

Russian Companies in the Forthcoming EU Member States: A Case of Lukoil in Bulgaria

Peter Zashev

SUMMARY. If serious problems of business ethics plague and continue to plague the way business is conducted within Russia, the internationalization of Russian companies puts forward the problem of what business culture they bring along and what impact it may have on the recipient country. This article focuses on the case of Lukoil investments and operations in Bulgaria. It describes the main factors forming the contemporary Russian business culture and highlights the negative features that could be feared from the point of view of the country receiving Russian investments. Later the paper tries to analyze the operations of Lukoil in Bulgaria and investigate if there is reason to suspect a negative business culture spillover. *[Article copies available for a fee from The Haworth Document Delivery Service: 1-800-HAWORTH. E-mail address: <docdelivery@haworthpress.com> Website: <http://www.HaworthPress.com> © 2005 by The Haworth Press, Inc. All rights reserved.]*

KEYWORDS. Russian investments in Bulgaria, Lukoil, Neftochim

Peter Zashev is Senior Research Fellow, Pan-European Institute, Turku School of Economics and Business Administration.

The author would like to thank Professor Kari Liuhto for the valuable comments and ideas expressed while reviewing an earlier version of this paper.

[Haworth co-indexing entry note]: "Russian Companies in the Forthcoming EU Member States: A Case of Lukoil in Bulgaria." Zashev, Peter. Co-published simultaneously in *Journal of East-West Business* (The Haworth Press, Inc.) Vol. 11, No. 3/4, 2005, pp. 109-128; and: *Expansion or Exodus: Why Do Russian Corporations Invest Abroad?* (ed: Kari Liuhto) The Haworth Press, Inc., 2005, pp. 109-128. Single or multiple copies of this article are available for a fee from The Haworth Document Delivery Service [1-800-HAWORTH, 9:00 a.m. - 5:00 p.m. (EST). E-mail address: docdelivery@haworthpress.com].

Available online at http://www.haworthpress.com/web/JEB

doi:10.1300/J097v11n03_09

INTRODUCTION

As of September 2004, Russian investments in Bulgaria were ranked only at 12th place amounting officially for USD 214 million (InvestBulgaria, 2004). This figure is somewhat unreliable as Russian investments are known also to come from destinations, such as the Netherlands (ranked 3rd), Cyprus (ranked 10th), and Luxembourg (ranked together with Belgium 6th). The Russian Embassy in Bulgaria estimates that Russian investments in Bulgaria amount to approximately USD 500 million as of 2004. Lukoil alone has invested into the Bulgarian economy over USD 340 million between 1999 and 2002 (Titov, 2004).

Thus the most tangible Russian investment came in late 1999 when Lukoil bought one of the largest companies in the country, the oil refinery Neftochim in Bourgas. The importance of Neftochim for the Bulgarian economy could be described with two figures: the oil refinery produces 9% of Bulgaria GDP and 25% of all taxes collected by the Bulgarian Government (Lukoil, 2003).

PRELIMINARY ASSUMPTIONS AND EMPLOYED METHOD

If serious problems of business ethics plague and continue to plague the way business is conducted within Russia, the internationalization of Russian companies puts forward several questions, such as:

1. What exactly business cultural influence do they spread when they internationalize?
2. Standardization or localization–do Russians use a standardized approach of utilizing Russian business culture or do they try to adapt to the local environment?
3. Is it correct to claim that Russian companies prefer Russian managers in their offices abroad?
4. Are the known negative features in Russian business ethics influencing other business cultures when the Russian corporations go abroad and if yes then to what extent?

While a large number of literature is dedicated to national business cultures in general and Russian business culture in particular, virtually none deal with the subject of what business culture Russian companies spread when they appear in the role of international investors. What could be assumed when one is considering reviewing and analyzing the business cultural impact of the Russian oil company Lukoil in Bulgaria?

To start with, Russian companies along their Chinese, Taiwanese and South Korean counterparts are seen as the most active bribers in international business (Transparency International, 2002). Lukoil comes from Russia and Russia takes the 90th position in the Transparency International 2004 Corruption Perception Index, along with countries such as India, Nepal and Tanzania. Bulgaria is listed in the aforementioned index as number 54 (Transparency International, 2004).

To summarize–when a company coming from a country with a flourishing corruption operates in a country that is not among the 50 least corrupted countries, one may not expect a positive mutual influence in terms of business ethics and corporate practices.

The business cultural influence of foreign investors is a subject that is still relatively unexplored by the cross-cultural management discipline. The main problem is how that influence could be qualified and quantified. There are many factors that should be considered. One is the size of the investor's home country and economy and the size of the country/economy-recipient of the investment. For instance, Lukoil's acquisition of Getty Petroleum marketing (gas stations chain) in the USA is unlikely to have significant cultural impact due to the geographic and economic size of the country recipient of the investment. On the other hand, the Russian investments in Latvia are more likely to have tangible impact in terms of business cultural impact as both Latvian geography and economy are considerably smaller (Zashev, 2005).

Another factor to be considered is how far apart are the investor's home country and the investor's host country in terms of national cultures. The latter could be described in terms of language, religion, ethnicity, shared history, etc. Or it could be compared in terms of a Hofstede analysis (1985). Last but not least the size of the investments should be also considered and measured not only in absolute terms but also in terms of their impact and importance for the economy of the host country.

In the absence of an established methodological instrument for measuring the cultural influence of an international investor, when reviewing Lukoil's investments in Bulgaria the paper will account the mentioned above factors and then will utilize a framework suggested by McCarthy and Puffer (2003) but somewhat modified by the author for the analysis of the Russian corporate governance.

The framework includes four components of the corporate governance as rectangles and three stakeholder groups as ovals. The authors stress that the system should be viewed as a system of interrelated forces, such that a change in any element affects others, while simultaneously affecting the primary stakeholders at the centre of the framework.

THE CONCERNS WITH RUSSIAN BUSINESS CULTURE

Factors Forming the Contemporary Business Culture

There are many studies dedicated to different aspects of Russian business culture, management. They are often focused more into some specific issue of Russian business culture. Some have a more general nature (Apressyan, 1997; Grachev & Izyumov, 2003; Kuznetsova & Kuznetsov, 2003), others focus on management perspectives (Ardichvilli et al., 1998; Liuhto, 1999; Robertson et al., 2003; De Vries et al., 2004), corporate governance (McCarthy & Puffer, 2002, 2003; Perotti & Gelfer, 2001) or some sadly specific issues for Russia such as corruption (Levin & Satarov, 2000). These are just a few of the many research papers published on the topic.

One way to describe the layers that form the contemporary Russian business culture is to unite them in four sets of factors. The contemporary Russian corporate culture could be presented as the cross-section of these four different sets of factors and their consequent impact on collective and individual culture and mentality.

The first set is formed by the traditional Russian values and norms that are distinctly Russian as compared to other national cultures. The second set could be defined as those norms and values that were added/enforced to the Russian mentality during the time of the Soviet Union. The third set represents those new developments and modifications in mentality and culture that the last 12 years of transition process required from every social group and/or individual in Russia. Finally, the fourth set of factors is assembled by the influence of Western business culture whose impact constantly increases due to the increased business interaction.

A brief critical survey of the four sets is provided below focusing on the influence they have had and the features they have brought to contemporary Russian corporate culture.

Commonly Russian Values and Morals

One of the most striking factors influencing the commonly Russian business values and morals could be defined as the near total lack of competition in the Russian social and economical life–an argument that was pointed out by many authors (e.g., Prohorov, 2002). Thus among the three main features were:

- *Militaristic nature* as the state had to fight external enemies and expand further geographically.
- *Society based on force rather than law* with clearly determined division of social groups. These groups differ by their duties rather than by their rights.
- *Supreme power of the state/tsar* with unclarified and unlimited authority space.

All these features were slowly suffocating the very concept of free competition in the allocation of any type of resources–human, financial, natural, etc. As a result a highly centralized system was built where the state in the face of the Russian emperor had unlimited and unclarified powers. The latter were transmitted to the rest through an ever growing, slow and inefficient apparatus of state bureaucracy. It is not a surprise that in such conditions the competitiveness was directed mainly on attracting the attention of the supreme power through gifts, bribes and a network of important acquaintances. That is how events such as the scandals of cronyism surrounding the close circle around Peter the Great or the 'Potemkin village' could be explained.

Such a system will also partially explain that all prominent international Russian business projects–be they in railways, investments or simple exports–were in most cases directly or indirectly sanctioned and/or financed by the state.

Soviet Values and Moral

The system did not change much in the Soviet era–instead to a fair degree it became worse. The state succeeded in implementing total control on all activities–control which could be characterized as deeper and broader if compared to the centralized administration during the tsar's times.

Again the state had the unclarified and unlimited authority to allocate resources of all types. Furthermore, the state imposed an ideological embargo that additionally stalled the system. The Soviet rule also imposed concepts such as the 'uravnilovka' that eliminated the link between work and pay, 'planning' versus market that geared further the bureaucracy and made cheating an inbuilt part of the economic system, 'repression' that became a state concept and thus eliminated initiative, decision making and freedom of choice.

Again, surviving and economic (and physical) prospering in the system was dependent on one's links to the state power in its various forms: communist party, state administration, military, KGB, etc. Again the competition was leveled down to none as most factories obtained a monopolist status and were given predetermined figures on input and output.

The Soviet system also did not succeed to eliminate the corruption and bribing that plagued the state machine in the times of the tsar. Quite the opposite, in the presence of an almost total deficit for goods and services corruption became the normal way of life. The basic lesson Soviet managers learned was that being obedient to the system through keeping a low profile was the best strategy to follow. Maximizing the requested from the planning committee input and minimizing the expected output was a common strategy.

The foreign operations of Soviet companies were an absolute state monopoly controlled by the party, the state and the KGB. Officially only the Foreign Trade Organizations were authorized to link Soviet factories with their overseas markets, suppliers, partners, etc. Any investment decision, be it a power plant in Cuba, a factory in Sudan or military equipment to Egypt, was part of a conscious centrally planned and controlled foreign policy rather than a money wise business rational based decision.

Transition Values and Moral

Perhaps the most interesting and intriguing period that has a considerable influence on the Russian business culture is the economic and political transition that Russia has been experiencing for the last 14 years.

A dramatic (by the Russian standards) change has appeared in the form of a massive (initial) retreat of the state. Dodgy or not, fair or not, the privatization in Russia created in a few years a new social group of owners–investors, capitalists, industrialists, etc. Still, it must be noticed that it was not their entrepreneurial spirit that was the main factor for their success. It was rather a well built network of contacts with the government at all different levels in combination with a total disrespect for the 'transitional' semi-Soviet, semi-market legal system. The state retreat in the 1990s and its inability to perform vital functions generated a huge vacuum in the economic and social situation in Russia. Russian managers at the time had to deal with a number of stressful forces.

One of them was the high inflation that was making business itself a difficult task and almost impossible to make any mid- or long-term business decisions and planning. Such a high degree of unpredictability was one of the main reasons for Russian managers to be focused mainly on short term incomes, profits, etc. Another reason for that was the absence of normal corporate banking (that still continues) and of bank credits to businesses. That meant that alternative sources of financing are needed. Such are typically very risky conditions and provided from very risky places.

Another serious obstacle was the growing organized crime that was constantly trying (and to a large degree succeeded) to be deeply involved in business. Drugs, prostitution and racketeering were only the initial operations that soon went into much more sophisticated schemes such as tax dodging, money laundering, banking and privatization. In the presence of next to no existing legal system and dysfunctional courts, business disputes and debt collection became a domain of activities for organized crime.

Not succeeding into building a stable macroeconomic environment, launching a failed bank reform, and not effectively combating organized crime were perhaps not the biggest shortcomings of the Russian State in the early 1990s. The worst three pressures that the state offered to businesses and managers were an extremely weak and corrupted institutional/bureaucratic machine, practically disabled courts and an unrealistic tax system that made most members of the business community outlaws by definition. Surprisingly, during the 1990s the state stopped performing vital duties of control and regulation but still remained the prior arbiter with the known from history unclarified and unlimited rights to interfere with everybody's business and daily life.

The Fear of Russian Business Culture

From the presented above evidence one may jump to the somewhat dark conclusion that Russian companies are some sort of puppets in the hands of the Russian State, that they bribe themselves out of any situation, rely mainly on informal networking, have overmanned and inefficient labor and managerial practices and generally in their survival mechanism there is little respect for law. To some extent this description may fit many Russian companies operating in Russia. But not all.

Hence, if serious problems of business ethics plague and continue to plague the way business is conducted within Russia, the internationalization of Russian companies puts forward the question exactly what business cultural influence do they spread when they internationalize? Standardization or localization–do Russian companies and executives use a standardized approach of utilizing Russian business culture or they try to adapt to the local environment? Is the statement that Russians see no problem with favoritism, price fixing, ignoring senseless laws and regulations and manipulating data (Puffer, 1996) valid and do they bring such a type of thinking in their foreign operations?

When it comes to their overseas operations the situation is a bit more complicated than that. The Russian companies are also acknowledged to be among the most active bribers when doing business abroad (Transparency International, 2002).

The discussed above assumptions provide enough reason to assume that as most worrying features of Russian corporate culture could be considered:

- An unbroken link/dependence of Russian companies on state and stemming from it consequences over political versus economic motivation when making corporate decisions.
- Non-negative attitude towards bribing and corruption.
- Transmitting dubious corporate management and organization with an accent on the somehow neglected in Russia issues of raising efficiency and productivity.

LUKOIL AS THE RUSSIAN MNC CHAMPION

General Background

The privatization plan was approved and first issue of Lukoil shares was registered. ConocoPhillips is not yet included among the shareholders even though that latest reports demonstrate that ConocoPhillips holds 10% and has received blocking control over key decisions at Lukoil following changes to the charter of the Russian firm (FSU Energy, 2005).

It is interesting to observe that the majority shares are presented by the banks/investment funds that play the role of nominee and do not reveal the true owners of the company. In January 2005, the Russian business magazine *Kommersant* presented a list of the richest Russians based on their official tax declarations. From the 33 officially richest persons, six are from the Lukoil Board of Directors or managers and officially hold in total 4% or approximately one billion US dollars.

The Fear Factor

In observing the Lukoil business culture and practices, one should investigate first if the formulated in the previous paragraph major negative features of Russian business culture could be found in the company's operational patterns and history.

Lukoil is a part of the Russian foreign policy instruments. To some extent that is normal as any government worldwide utilizes its big business champions in foreign politics. The two arising questions are: (1) to what extent the utilization could be considered normal and (2) if the government will respect the rules or will re-write them just as with the case of Yukos.

At present, Lukoil is approved by the Kremlin. Its CEO, Vagit Alekperov, is in good standing with the president, Vladimir Putin. In July 2004, the Russian president, the ConocoPhillips CEO and Alekperov discussed oil and gas projects during a meeting in the Krasnodar territory (Interfax, 23.07.2004). Russia's Minister for Industry and Energy, Viktor Khristenko, described the Russia-driven integration of energy systems in the former Soviet republics as "*an instrument of solving political issues in the CIS*" (Gateway to Russia, April 27th 2004).

Still, only a few years ago the Russian tax police have simultaneously opened criminal charges against Lukoil and Alekperov for concealing revenues in "*especially large amounts*" (GPF, 2000). The 1995 scandal surrounding Lukoil and its practice of mixing different gasoline types that brought them an additional profit of 4.6 billion rubles can easily be brought back (Rstaki, 1999). Bureaucrats are who covered it back then and bureaucrats are who can easily bring it up again, just as in the Yukos case. Is it then possible to foresee if Lukoil will always stay as a favorite to the Russian Government? And if not, is it possible to claim that Lukoil is a competitive, stable, and predictable international player?

In terms of corruption and bribing it is not easy to say if Lukoil is more involved or less involved than the average international oil company. One factor to be considered is that its managerial board consists predominantly of Russians who have been born, raised and educated in Russia. Thus on a general level one may assume that they have a more flexible understanding of the acceptability of bribing as a business instrument or about corruption in general, especially in a country such as Russia whose business environment is so dependent on lobbying with all possible and impossible means the state bureaucracy.

The patchy set of facts one hears here and there may only confirm the above assumptions. The most damaging perhaps recent scandal that involves Lukoil is the unsuccessful bid for the privatization of the Gdansk Refinery in Poland. There is an ongoing parliamentary investigation of the circumstances that sound more like a spy novel: former KGB agent, Lukoil, high Polish officials and bribes (TemletonThorp, 2004). The US report on the Saddam Hussein oil vouchers scheme in the oil for food also lists Lukoil as a recipient of 63 million barrels of Iraqi crude oil (Smith & Lynch, 2004). What is amazing is that against the size and financial strength of Lukoil it is truly a small amount.

LUKOIL'S OPERATIONS IN BULGARIA

Primary Stakeholders

Shareholders

Lukoil participated in the privatization procedure for the Bulgarian oil refinery Neftochim in 1999 and won the tender offering some USD 100 million for 58% and investing USD 400 million to modernize the refining complex. The Russian investor pledged also to take on the Neftochim debt of USD 230 million (BGN420 million). The other bidders included Balkan Oil that was a consortium including Yukos Oil and Petrol Holding, and four Russian energy companies: Rosneft, Slavneft, Orel Oil and Trans-stroygaz. An adviser to the deal was the international consulting company Arthur Andersen (*Financial Times*, Oct. 13 1999, 34). As a part of the privatization procedure the government kept a 'golden share,' i.e., share which enables it to exercise control over Neftochim. The golden share proved enough to ensure the Bulgarian Government that the refinery as a strategic asset will be monitored and controlled by the state even if in private hands.

The relations of Lukoil Neftochim Bourgas with its minority shareholders were not always smooth. Vostok Nafta investment bank possessed at the time six per cent from the Bulgarian Lukoil Neftochim Bourgas and accused the Russian Lukoil that it "*artificially decreased the revenues and the profitability of the Bulgarian company using transfer prices.*" In 2002, the portfolio manager of Vostok-Nafta Pert Brilioth commented further that "*Lukoil did not meet the expectations of the minority shareholders.*" In his opinion, the Lukoil activities helped for the Lukoil Neftochim Bourgas capitalization at the time to be less than USD 50 million; that was too low a figure for a refinery of such size (*Kommersant*, 2002).

At the end of 2004, Lukoil Europe Holdings B.V. (a 100% subsidiary of Lukoil) purchased the shares owned by minority shareholders of Lukoil Neftochim Bourgas. The tender offered to buy 29% shares at BGN 28 per share was announced in December 2004 and approved by the Financial Supervision Commission of Bulgaria. According to the tender results, owners of 22% of the refinery accepted the tender offer and thus the Lukoil Europe Holdings B.V. share in the capital of Lukoil Neftochim Bourgas reached 93% (Lukoil, 2005).

Board of Directors and Management

At the centre of the model are positioned the primary stakeholders and their interrelations. These are top managers, shareholders, and boards of directors–groups that decide upon, implement and execute corporate governance in Russian corporations.

It could be noted that while the entire management body of Lukoil Bulgaria (8 managers) consists of Bulgarian nationals (Appendix 1), the situation somewhat changes when it comes to the value adding part of the company, namely Lukoil Neftochim Bourgas.

In the Supervisory Board of the latter is its Chairman, Dmitrii Tarasov, who is also Vice-President of Lukoil. The appointment of such a high ranking officer from the Lukoil headquarters could be interpreted as a sign of the importance the mother company gives to the Bulgarian refinery. A member of the Supervisory Board is yet another prominent figure from Lukoil headquarters, Vladimir Rakitski, who was also a former CEO of Lukoil Neftochim Bourgas. The Supervisory Board includes also three Bulgarian nationals. These are Dimitar Ivanovski, who is Deputy Minister for the Economy and thus represents the state, Christo Hadjikolev, who is also former managing director of Neftochim Bourgas and represents the minority shareholders interests, and finally Wilhelm Kraus, who is Deputy General Director of Lukoil Bulgaria (Ibid.).

The Board of Directors of Lukoil Neftochim Bourgas is chaired by Valentin Zlatev, who is also General Manager of Lukoil Bulgaria, and includes two Russian and two Bulgarian members. The Russians are the refinery CEO Igor Kuzmin and what could be considered the financial controller from Lukoil Europe Holding, Alexei Belobragin. The Bulgarian members of the board are managers in Litasco (Lukoil International Trading and Supply Company–Litasco) Bulgaria that is 100% owned by Lukoil (Ibid.).

It is notable that despite the majority of Bulgarian nationals in the company management, most key positions are clearly assigned to Russian nationals. The strongest authority in terms of supervision and overall control lies directly with the Vice-President of Lukoil. The main value added process, i.e., refining crude oil, is handled by Igor Kuzmin. Finally the control, management and supervision of financial flows are in the hands of Alexei Belobragin from the holding company Lukoil Europe Holdings. Valentin Zlatev made a career in the Russian oil industry and reached the level of vice-president of Rosneft before moving to Lukoil Bulgaria.

The most controversial figure in the top layer of Lukoil Bulgaria is Wilhelm Kraus. He was deputy mayor of Sofia (1992-1997) and Minister of Transportation (1997-1999) in the government of Ivan Kostov. His name is involved in a number of economic scandals in Bulgaria and he is currently being prosecuted for economic mismanagement during his tenure as a minister.

Secondary Stakeholders

Among the secondary stakeholders listed are the employees, creditors, customers and suppliers. Lukoil Bulgaria proves to be one of the most respected employers in Bulgaria. The average salary in Lukoil is among the highest in Bulgaria. The employees of Lukoil Bulgaria are also among the very few in Bulgaria that are included in corporate pension funds. As mentioned above the company has an international certificate in occupational health and safety management

Lukoil Bulgaria is not known as a major debtor. The company could be in debt to Lukoil but there is no information of its exact volume. The main supplier of Lukoil Bulgaria is Lukoil Neftochim Bourgas. The main supplier to Lukoil Neftochim Bourgas is Litasco Bulgaria, which on their account are owned by Litasco Switzerland that is owned by Lukoil. Thus on the supply side the company is fully integrated and does not really interact with outsiders.

Lukoil Bulgaria's approach to handling customers deserves more attention. Here the company is clearly pursuing a multi-track strategy. The main exporter of Lukoil Neftochim Bourgas products is Litasco Bulgaria. Another part of the strategy is the development and expansion of their own retail network that includes also a chain of gas stations.

Currently, there are almost 3,000 petrol and gas stations in Bulgaria. Petrol's network is the biggest, with 375 filling stations, followed by Lukoil, with 120 stations, and Shell and OMV, with 82 and 69 stations respectively. Aggregate sales in 2004 of the four biggest companies are almost equal to those of all the rest. Petrol is the leader with a 18% market share, followed by Lukoil–12%, Shell–10%, and OMV–nine per cent (Banker, Dec 31st 2004).

In December 2004, Lukoil Bulgaria also paid BGN 84 million for 18% in Petrol AD (the largest gas station owner with over 400 gas stations). It is clear that Lukoil Bulgaria has the ambition to continue the vertical integration process and establish itself as one of the main retailers of fuels and gasoline. That will mean in some future dealings with customers for Lukoil Bulgaria could mean mainly end customers.

Peripheral Stakeholders

Arthur Andersen was the consultant in the privatization of Neftochim Bourgas oil refinery. The Raiffeisenbank helped the company announce a tender and consolidate its shares in 2004. Lukoil is listed on the London Stock Exchange which is a positive sign when it comes to the openness and transparency of the company. Moody's Investors Service assigned at the end of 2003 a Ba2 senior implied and a Ba3 issuer rating to Lukoil. The company's rating outlook is stable. Moody's rating is one grade higher than that of Standard & Poor's (Capital Link, 2003). KPMG conducts Lukoil audits since 1995 and the company's financial results are published under the US Generally Accepted Accounting Principles (GAAP).

Technology and Environment

In 2001, the US Trade and Development Agency extended a USD 450,000 grant to help fund a feasibility study of a modernization study for Neftochim. The agreement was signed by the then director of Neftochim and the then US ambassador in Bulgaria (TDA, 2001).

Lukoil Neftochim invested in 2002 USD 64 million that was 20% more than expected. The company netted only a relatively small profit of EUR 2 million for the year but managed to repay some EUR 170 million in arrears to the state budget dating back to before its privatization in 1999 (EIU, 2003).

In October 2003, Lukoil Neftochim Bourgas received the international certificates for environmental management and occupational health and safety management systems with the international standards ISO 14001:1996 and OHSAS 18001:1999. The company also holds a quality standard certificate ISO 9001:2000. Lukoil Neftochim

Bourgas is also aiming to comply with and receive certificates for information management systems (ISO 17799/BS 7799), social responsibility (SA 8000) and human resources management (Investor in People) (Club9000, 2003).

By the end of 2004, the major reconstruction of the main production facilities was finished and the total size of Lukoil in Lukoil Neftochim Bourgas reached some USD 400 million. The results include 40% increase of the production capacity and an increase in the production of high octane gasoline as well as a reduction in the sulphur emissions.

In June 2004, Lukoil Neftochim Bourgas report revealed that the company succeeded in reduce emissions by 22%. As to the end of 2004, it is expected that as a result of the upgrade program the refinery will turn to EURO-3 standards in 2007 and EURO-4 standards in 2009 (Lukoil, 2005).

Lukoil plans to spend USD 400 million by 2012 on upgrading the 160,000 b/d Neftochim refinery, according to Alekperov. The investments will aim at bringing the production requirements in compliance with EU standards and regulations (*NEFTE Compass*, 2004).

Legal and Political

Lukoil Bulgaria is too important a company and too important an economic asset to be neglected or passively treated by the government. The Bulgarian Government keeps control through the 'golden share' and is thus represented in the board of directors of Lukoil Neftochim Bourgas.

The interaction between Lukoil and the Bulgarian Government did not start smoothly. In February 1999, the Bulgarian privatization agency and Arthur Andersen denied the right of Lukoil to participate in the tender for the sale of the state-owned Petrol company (Naryshkin, 1999). It later appeared to be a battle not with the Bulgarian Government but with Russian rivals who appeared to be lobbying more actively.

On its part Lukoil really did have a careful and balanced stance on all issues related to its operations in Bulgaria. As early as April 1999, when asked about the possibilities to invest into the Neftochim, Alekperov answered that "*I shall not speak of our desire to make this move until technological and economic examination of this purchase is made. Everything has its price and this price should be objective.*" April 1999 was also when Lukoil opened its first gas station–the first tangible investment of the company in Bulgaria (BBC, 1999).

For the 5 years of active operations in Bulgaria, Lukoil was not really involved into any big tensions or disputes with the government or of legal matters. As Alekperov put it, "*We evaluate our activities in Bulgaria to be Lukoil's most successful overseas project*" (Lukoil Press, 2004).

Social and Cultural Traditions

From the discusson above one may really assume that Lukoil could really be proud with the development of its Lukoil Bulgaria affiliate. However, the concern over continuity of business ethics and cultural traditions still remains. Lukoil was created in the shadows of the post-Soviet economic chaos in Russia by a high-ranking Soviet bureaucrat that is the company's current president. Even if it sincerely wished not to, it was still part of the turbulent and sometimes even violent transitional Russian business environment. The mysterious death of Vitaly Shmidt, its vice-president, in 1997 and the kidnapping of another one, Sergei Kukura, in 2002 were dark episodes of the company's history.

If Yukos was ruined for tax fraud, one should note that Lukoil was using the same tax evasion schemes. The Polish episode also reveals that Lukoil could use various instruments of persuasion if needed. The receipt of oil from Saddam Hussein was also a low moment in Lukoil history. In 2004, Lukoil Bulgaria's president, Valentin Zlatev, was chosen as a Bulgarian businessman of the year but one should remember that as a former vice-president of Rosneft he is also not alien to the particularities of the Russian business culture, including its negative sides. The appointed to the Board of Directors in January 2005 Oleksii Yurevich Belinki has also some murky records in his previous position as a deputy general director of Lukoil Ukraine (Kievskie Vedomosti, March 18th 2003).

All these moments in history, cultural traditions and the resulting ethical values serve as a warning that much should be done before Russian companies in general and Lukoil in particular will not be prejudiced and feared in their quality of international business actors.

CONCLUSIONS

This article reviewed what patterns of business culture and corporate governance Lukoil demonstrated in Bulgaria against what could be perceived as the negative side of the Russian business culture. Lukoil Bulgaria and Lukoil Neftochim Bourgas oil refinery are among the largest and most important economic players in the Bulgarian economy.

The company heavily invested in upgrading its facilities and achieved increased production output, better efficiency and an improved environmental record. The employees of Lukoil Bulgaria receive one of the highest salaries in the country and are covered by a corporate pension fund. The company is also in very good relations with the government, which is also presented in the Board of Directors and holds a controlling 'golden share' as an instrument of securing the state interests. Lukoil Bulgaria is continuing its expansion and investment program in Bulgaria and was praised by the Lukoil's president as one of the company's most successful international ventures, while Lukoil Bulgaria's president Valentin Zlatev was chosen as a businessman of the year in 2004.

Therefore, it would not be correct that the main concerns of dealing with the particularities of the Russian business culture were confirmed based on the case of Lukoil's operations in Bulgaria. Its link to the Russian Government is strong but that was not blatantly used or manifested during its operations in Bulgaria. To some extent perhaps Lukoil Bulgaria is an instrument of the Russian Government in the upcoming Bourgas-Alexandroupolis oil pipeline project, but that will be the case with any oil company and its native government when projects of such magnitude are at stake.

Utilizing corruption or bribery as a business instrument is something that at least secondary sources cannot confirm. The company is quite transparent by the Russian or Bulgarian standards and is generally transparent by the international standards.

The secondary data collected and presented above may conclude that Lukoil Bulgaria is an example of a Russian investor who is really trying to be a role model and that is an ambition that should be only encouraged. However, refining the theoretical model and using primary data such as questionnaires and interviews could considerably improve the quality of the research.

REFERENCES

Alexandrova Galina (2001) Sdelkata Lukoil–Naftex: pazarna strategia ili hod za oceliavane, *Kapital Weekly*, Sofia, Bulgaria, 30.06-06.07.2001, p. 32 (in Bulgarian)

Apressyan Ruben G. (1997) Business Ethics in Russia, *Journal of Business Ethics*, Volume 16, October 1997, pg. 1561.

Ardichvilli Alexander, Cardozo Richard N., Gasparishvilli Alexander (1998) Leadership styles and management practices of Russian entrepreneurs: Implications for transferability of Western HRD interventions, *Human Resource Development Quarterly*, Volume 9, Issue 2/1998, pg. 145-156.

Banker (2004) Petrol stations to be on the offensive in 2005 again, Dec 31st 2004, [cited 12 January 2005]. Available from World Wide Web: *<http://www.banker.bg/article.asp?artno=29&date=2004/12/31&issue=52&category=7>*.

BBC Monitoring Former Soviet Union (1999) Filling stations launches Russian oil company's investment drive in Bulgaria, London, Apr 15th, 1999. p. 1.

Capital Link (2003) MOODY's investor service assigns ratings to Lukoil, October 8th 2003, [cited 12 January 2005]. Available from World Wide Web: *<http://www.capitallinkrussia.com/press/companies/50010142/24791.html>*.

Club9000 (2003) Naj goliamata rafineria na balkanskia poluostrov sertificirana ot BVQ1 za kachestvo, ekologia I bezopasnost, 11 2003, [cited 12 January 2005]. Available from World Wide Web: *<www.club9000.org/news/lukoil2.asp>* (in Bulgarian).

De Vries Manfred K., Shekhsnia Stanislav, Korotov Konstantin, Florent Treacy (2004) The New Russian Global Leaders: Lessons from a Decade of Transition, *European Management Journal*, Volume 22, No. 6./December 2004, pp. 637-648.

EIU ViewsWire (2003) Bulgaria Industry: Lukoil invested US$64 million in local operations in 2002, New York, July 21, 2003.

FSU Energy (2005) ConoPhillips gains influencer at Lukoil, *Petroleum Argus*, Volume X/4, January 28th 2005.

Gateway to Russia (2005) Russia's economic diplomacy, April 27th 2005, [cited 12 January 2005]. Available from World Wide Web: *<http://www.gateway2russia.com/st/art_231868.php>*.

Global Policy Forum/GPF/ (2000) The Dilemma of Russia's Anti-Corruption Campaign, 13.07.2000, [cited 12 January 2005]. Available from World Wide Web: *<http://www.globalpolicy.org/nations/corrupt/russia3.htm>*.

Grachev Mikhail, Izyumov Alexei (2003) Development of Business Culture in a Newly Market Economy, *Journal of East-West Business*, Volume 9/2003, pg. 7-28.

Hofstede Geert (1985) The interaction between national and organizational value systems, *Journal of Management Studies*, N22, 1985, pp. 347-357.

Interfax (2004) Oil, gas projects discussed with Putin-Alekperov, 23.07.2004, at.

Invest Bulgaria Statistics (2004) Foreign direct investment inflow in Bulgaria by country and by year in USD million, [cited 12 January 2005]. Available from World Wide Web: *<http://www.investbg.government.bg/340/page.html>*.

Kievslkie Vedomosti (2003) Lukoil Ukraina–po belenkomu, March 18th 2003, [cited 12 January 2005]. Available from World Wide Web: *<http://www.kv.com.ua/index.php?rub=21&number_old=2862>*.

Kommersant (2002) Anglijskie aksionery zhaluiutsia na Lukoil, 19.01.2002 (in Russian).

Kuznetsova Olga, Kuznetsov A. (2003) Business Culture in Modern Russia: Deterrents and Influences, *Problems and Methods of Management*, No. 2, Kiev, 2003.

Levin Mark, Satarov Georgy (2000) Corruption and Institutions in Russia, *European Journal of Political Economy*, Volume 16, 2000, p. 113-132.

Liuhto Kari (1999) The Transformation of Management Effectiveness in the Post-Soviet Enterprises, *Journal for East European Management Studies*, 4/3, Chemnitz (1999) pp. 22.

Lukoil Press Release (2005) Lukoil increases its interest in the share capital of Bourgas refinery, 13.01.2005, [cited 12 January 2005]. Available from World Wide Web: *<http://www.lukoil.com/press_6_5div__id_21_1id_22309_.html>*.

Lukoil Press (2004) Lukoil i agenstvo po investiciam v Bolgarii prishli k vzaimpoponimaniu, October 2004, [cited 12 January 2005]. Available from World Wide Web: *<http://www.sf-online.ru/pressrelease.asp?OID=6F4A81BA-C8DE-44B1-B2B5-58FDBDCC83FB&sectionOID=&rubricOID=>*.

McCarthy Daniel J., Puffer Sheila M. (2003) Corporate governance in Russia: A framework for analysis, *Journal of World Business*, Volume 38, 2003, p. 397-415.

McCarthy Daniel J., Puffer Sheila M. (2002) Corporate governance in Russia: Toward a European, US or Russian Model?, *European Management Journal*, Volume 20, No. 6/December 2002, pg. 630-640.

Naryshkin Andrey (1999) Lukoil denied tender participation, *ITAR TASS News Wire*. New York, Feb 25 1999, pg. 1

NEFTE Compass (2004) Bulgaria: Lukoil Seeks To Swallow the Black Sea Refinery, London, Nov 3, 2004, pg. 1.

Perotti Enrico C., Gelfer Stanislav (2001) Red barons or robber barons? Governance and investment in Russian financial-industrial groups, *European Economic Review*, Volume 45/2001, pg. 1601-1617.

Prohorov A.P. (2002) Russkaja Model Upravlenia, A.P. Zhurnal Ekspert 2002, (in Russian).

Puffer Sheila M. (1996) Business and Management in Russia, Edward Elgar Pub, August 1996.

Robertson Christopher J., Gilley K., Street Marc D. (2003) The relationship between ethics and firm practices in Russia and the United States, *Journal of World Business*, Volume 38/2003, p. 375-384.

Rstaki Arsen (1999) Mir skazok Ole-Lukoile, *Novaja gazeta*, 20.12.1999 (in Russian)

Smith Jeffrey R. and Lynch Colum (2004) 1,300 Oil Vouchers Begin to Tell Story. Hussein Courted A World of Nations, Firms, Individuals, *Washington Post*, Friday, October 8, 2004; page A30.

TempletonThorp (2004) Secret Service Note names President in spy scandal, 2004, [cited 12 January 2005]. Available from World Wide Web: *<http://www.templetonthorp.com/en/news805>*.

Titov V. (2004) Equal rights for Russian investors, *Interview with HE Vl. Titov, Ambassador of Russia in Bulgaria,* October-November 2004, [cited 12 January 2005]. Available from World Wide Web: *<http://www.in-business.info/English/11En/new_page_8.htm>*.

Trade and Development Agency (2001) TDA Signs over $800,000 in Grants for Three Feasibility Studies in Bulgaria, *Trade & Export News*, 27 July 2001, [cited 12 January 2005]. Available from World Wide Web: *<http://www.tda.gov/trade/press/july27a_01.html>*.

Transparency International (2002) Bribe Payers Index, Russian, Chinese, Taiwanese and South Korean Companies, widely seen using bribes in developing countries, May 2002, [cited 12 January 2005]. Available from World Wide Web: *<http://www.transparency.org>*.

Transparency International (2004) Corruption Perceptions Index 2004, [cited 12 January 2005]. Available from World Wide Web: *<http://www.transparency.org/pressreleases_archive/2004/2004.10.20.cpi.en.html>*.

Zashev Peter (2005) Russian investments in Latvia–size, quality and business cultural impact, submitted in *Journal of Business Economics and Management*, February 2005.

Zashev Peter (2004) Russian investments in Lithuania–politics, business, corporate culture, *Electronic Publications of the Pan-European Institute*, 10/2004, Turku School of Economics and Business Administration.

APPENDIX 1

Structure of Supervisory Board, Board of Directors and Managerial Board at Lukoil Neftochim Bulgaria

Lukoil Bulgaria

Managerial Board

Valentin Zlatev	PhD., General Manager
Martin Ganev	First Deputy General Manager in Economics and Finance
Vasil Slavov	Deputy General Manager/Sales
Wilhelm Kraus	Deputy General Manager/Transport
Diana Damianova	Deputy General Manager/PR and Advertisement
Peter Vassilev	Administrative Director
Emil Kosturkov	Director Exploitation and Retail Dept.
Eng. Christoslav Todorov	Director Investments and Constructions

Lukoil Neftochim Bourgas

Supervisory Board

Chairman:	**Dmitrii Tarasov,** First Vice-President of Lukoil
Members:	**Vladimir Rakitskii,** Head of the Main Department for Oil Refining and Petrochemicals of Oil Company Lukoil **Dimitar Ivanovski,** Deputy Minister of Economy **Christo Hadjikolev** Representative of the small shareholders **Wilhelm Kraus** Deputy General Manager of Lukoil Bulgaria

Board of Directors

Chairman:	**Valentin Zlatev,** General Manager of Lukoil Bulgaria
Members:	**Ivan Yankov,** Manager Crude Oil Deliveries Litasco **Aleksey Belobragin,** Senior Expert Budgets and planning of Lukoil Europe holdings **Alexander Tchaouchev** Manager Litasco Bulgaria **Igor Kuzmin,** Chief Executive Officer of Lukoil Neftochim Bourgas

Russian Telecommunication Company MTS Goes to the CIS

Nikita E. Lisitsyn
Sergei F. Sutyrin
Olga Y. Trofimenko
Irina V. Vorobieva

SUMMARY. The article deals with the outward internationalization of Russia's telecommunication company Mobile TeleSystems (MTS). This research investigates both target foreign markets and entry strategies of the company. In 2002, MTS started with entries to Belarus and Ukraine, followed by expanding to Uzbekistan and Turkmenistan in 2004. The choice of CIS countries was determined by knowledge of business environment and practices which are similar to Russia, and by economic and political ties inherited from the past. The basic strategy was acquisition of local mobile operators with the exception of Belarus where a joint venture was established. The article suggests that new market entries are expected.

Nikita E. Lisitsyn is Lecturer, Sergei F. Sutyrin is Professor and the Head of the Department, Olga Y. Trofimenko is Associate Professor, and Irina V. Vorobieva is Associate Professor, all at the Department of World Economy, St. Petersburg State University, Russia.

[Haworth co-indexing entry note]: "Russian Telecommunication Company MTS Goes to the CIS." Lisitsyn, Nikita E. et al. Co-published simultaneously in *Journal of East-West Business* (The Haworth Press, Inc.) Vol. 11, No. 3/4, 2005, pp. 129-147; and: *Expansion or Exodus: Why Do Russian Corporations Invest Abroad?* (ed: Kari Liuhto) The Haworth Press, Inc., 2005, pp. 129-147. Single or multiple copies of this article are available for a fee from The Haworth Document Delivery Service [1-800-HAWORTH, 9:00 a.m. - 5:00 p.m. (EST). E-mail address: docdelivery@haworthpress.com].

Available online at http://www.haworthpress.com/web/JEB

doi:10.1300/J097v11n03_10

KEYWORDS. Internationalization of a Russian firm, telecommunication, MTS

COMPANY BACKGROUND

MTS is the largest telecom service provider in Russia, operating in GSM standard. In Russia, the number of its subscribers exceeds 26 million as for the beginning of 2005. Having licenses to provide telecom services in 87 Russian regions (out of 88) the company currently runs its operations in 61 regions. In the third quarter of 2004, the revenue of MTS totaled over one billion US dollars, net profits approached USD 340 million and EBITDA was over USD 630 million. Its market capitalization amounted to USD 13 billion by the end of 2004.

MTS began its operations in October, 1993. The company was founded by the Moscow fixed-line operator MGTS (Moscow City Telephone Network) and several other domestic shareholders, on the one side, and DeTeMobil (Deutsche Telecom's subsidiary) and Siemens, on the other side, as a closed joint stock company. The Russian and the German shareholders owned 53% and 47% in the company, respectively. In early 1995, AFK Sistema, a Moscow-based financial group, consolidated the stakes of Russian shareholders; at the same time, DeTeMobil purchased Siemens' stake. The history of MTS as a public company began in 2000 with IPO on the US market.

The latest changes in MTS ownership structure took place in the end of 2004, when Deutsche Telekom sold 15% of Mobile TeleSystems on the off-board market. At the moment, the controlling stock belongs to AFK Sistema while the share of Deutsche Telecom (now represented by T-Mobile company) decreased down to 10%. Nearly one per cent of the company's shares belong to its management. The rest is traded on NYSE, European off-board markets and MMVB (Moscow Interbank Currency Exchange).

MTS is number one among the three largest telecom service providers in Russia. Its market share equals to 35%. Two other leaders–VimpelCom and MegaFon–control 34% and 19% of the market correspondingly.

According to the European Mobile Communications (EMC) Report, the total amount of telecom service subscribers in Russia in all standards has reached 56 million people by the end of the third quarter of 2004 (EMC, 2004). The Russian market provides more than 70% of the mobile service subscribers in the former Soviet republics. Average penetration rate in Russia equals to almost 40%. It means that there are still quite good opportunities for Russian companies to expand inside the market of the former USSR.

At the same time in Russia the difference between the regions is really large. On the one hand, Moscow with penetration more than 71% and St. Petersburg with 60% are quite similar to Japan or the USA. On the other hand, in about twenty regions penetration rate is still below 10%. More than that, one could expect that in the medium run regional disparity will remain substantial enough. A certain trend towards convergence might occur, resulting from more intensive competition both in the most developed areas and in other parts of the country.

MTS' GENERAL APPROACH TO NEW MARKET ENTRY

During 1993-2001, MTS was developing on the domestic market, increasing its coverage area by regional expansion within Russia. In 2002-2004 the company started its internationalization by expanding to neighboring CIS countries. For any company in the mobile communication sector, entering the new national market means the extending of its network largely through the usage of existing infrastructure in the country of destination. From that point of view, the higher the level of its technological development the more attractive is the target market. This factor also strongly favors acquisitions of existing companies, which operate on the local mobile communications market and have their own infrastructure and subscriber base. In addition to that, a regulatory factor is rather important for mobile communications sector as the state (in particular due to security reasons) quite often tries to protect it from foreign operators. In general, a combination of technological and regulatory considerations largely predetermines foreign market entry mode for the companies in the sector.

MTS started its internationalization in several neighboring CIS countries. The main reasons for choosing these target markets related to historical and cultural traditions, common infrastructure network inherited from the Soviet era, and relatively similar business practices. In addition to that one should take under consideration geographical proximity, which clearly favored expansion towards close neighbors. At the same time, in this case it is a rather controversial issue as several target markets (for example, Uzbekistan) are located relatively far from main Russian economic centers.

Integration within the CIS is a priority political target for Russia. Despite all the difficulties, political relations between most of the CIS countries tend to develop positively. Considering the large role of the state in the mobile communications sector this political ties favor co-operation, help Russian companies to penetrate regulatory frontiers (that is especially important in cases of Belarus, Uzbekistan and Turkmenistan). Moreover, internationalization to CIS countries for MTS actually fits the 'follow your consumer' strategy. Many Russian companies being MTS corporate clients have already entered markets of CIS countries and actively develop economic co-operation in the area. Human migration within the CIS is also an important reason, as it formed an initial basis as well as incentive for internationalization by enhancing co-operation between mobile operators from Russia and other CIS countries (supplying international roaming services).

Overall mobile service subscriber base in the CIS and the Baltic States today exceeds 75 million people.[1] The region is a fast developing market where the competition is still rather modest, while the opportunities are substantial. All these countries are transitional economies and the former USSR republics. They all started the transition process right after obtaining their sovereignty in 1992. After a dramatic decline in the 1990s, nearly all the economies experienced a rapid growth during the last five years. Markets of this area, however, do not form an entity, as they differ tremendously from each other both by subscriber base potential and by current penetration level (see Table 1).

The Baltic States are the leaders in the region under review in terms of penetration level. In Estonia the penetration reached almost 85%; in Lithuania it is about 80% and in Latvia 65%. Taking into consideration the relatively small population of these countries, high level of competition, and the fact that market positions of the already operating telecom companies are relatively strong, Russian mobile service providers have not that much incentive to enter these markets today. Another important factor relates to the recent EU enlargement. After joining the Union, the Baltic States introduced its rules and regulations on their territory. That creates additional barriers for the expansion of Russian companies.

Substantial heterogeneity of mobile communication services markets in the CIS countries mainly results from current variety in standards of living. For example, Russia has GDP per capita 15 times higher than Tajikistan (see Table 2). Large and potentially promising markets like Uzbekistan have low penetration level first and foremost due to the poverty of the majority of the population and absence of middle class.

TABLE 1. Mobile Subscribers in the CIS

Country	Number of subscribers, September 2004	Change in number of subscribers (%), September 2004/ September 2003	Penetration rate (%), September 2004
Armenia	150,600	80.1	4.5
Azerbaijan	1,419,400	32.8	18.0
Belarus	1,856,300	115.4	18.0
Georgia	893,700	43.7	18.2
Kazakhstan	2,203,600	86.5	13.1
Kyrgyzstan	247,200	161.0	5.0
Moldova	654,700	49.1	14.7
Russia	56,106,140	88.6	39.0
Tajikistan	95,180	637.3	1.4
Turkmenistan	13,650	35.0	0.3
Ukraine	10,299,100	116.7	21.6
Uzbekistan	467,100	91.5	1.8

Source: Calculated from EMC (2003; 2004).

TABLE 2. Basic Macroeconomic Indicators of CIS Countries

	Territory, thousand square km	Population, million	GDP per capita, 2003, USD	GDP growth (%)					
				1998	1999	2000	2001	2002	2003
Russia	17,075.2	143.4	3,023.0	−5.3	6.4	10.0	5.1	4.7	7.3
Ukraine	603.7	48.4	1,022.7	−1.9	−0.2	5.9	9.2	4.8	8.5
Uzbekistan	447.4	25.6	386.7	4.4	4.4	3.8	4.5	4.2	4.4
Kazakhstan	2,717.3	14.9	1,993.3	−1.9	2.7	9.8	13.5	9.8	9.2
Belarus	207.6	9.9	1,767.7	8.3	3.4	5.8	4.7	5.0	6.8
Azerbaijan	86.6	8.2	865.9	10.0	7.4	11.1	9.9	10.6	11.2
Tajikistan	143.1	6.3	206.4	5.3	3.7	8.3	10.2	9.5	10.2
Kyrgyzstan	198.5	5.1	333.3	2.1	3.7	5.4	5.3	0.0	6.7
Georgia	69.7	5.1	764.7	3.1	2.9	1.8	4.8	5.5	8.6
Turkmenistan	488.1	4.9	1,224.5	...	...	...	...	...	16.9
Moldova	33.8	4.2	476.2	−6.5	−3.4	2.1	6.1	7.8	6.3
Armenia	29.8	3.1	903.2	7.2	3.3	5.9	9.6	12.9	13.9

Sources: Intergovernmental Statistical Committee of the CIS Countries (2005); World Bank (2005).

Several large companies dominate the telecom market of the CIS and the Baltic States. Relevant information is depicted in Table 3. The table shows that MTS being the leader on the Russian market at the same time manages to enter more foreign countries than any of its main competitors.

Belarus

Belarus happened to be the first CIS target destination for MTS. With its population of nearly 10 million, Belarus is the fifth largest country of the alliance. The population density is some 50 people per sq. km. GDP growth varied from 3% in 1999 to 7% in 2003. In 2003, GDP per capita amounted to close USD 1,800 (the third place among the CIS countries).

Belarus has lagged behind most East European transition countries in developing mobile communications. It was the last state in the region to introduce GSM cellular digital standard, having relied between 1993 and 1999 on an analogue cellular phone service. Mobile phone penetration has nevertheless increased rapidly in recent years. In particular, it more than doubled from September 2003 to September 2004, and has reached the level of about 20% with approximately two million mobile subscribers. Meanwhile, the potential of the Belarus cellular market has

TABLE 3. Ten Leading Mobile Services Providers in the CIS and the Baltic States

Company	Country of origin	Countries of operation
MTS	Russia	Russia, Belarus, Ukraine, Uzbekistan, Turkmenistan
VimpelCom	Russia	Russia, Kazakhstan
MegaFon	Russia	Russia, Tajikistan
Fintur	Netherlands	Kazakhstan, Azerbaijan, Georgia, Moldova
TELE2	Sweden	Russia, Latvia, Lithuania, Estonia
Kyivstar	Ukraine	Ukraine
Uralsvjasiform	Russia	Russia
SMARTS	Russia	Russia
Omnitel	USA	Lithuania
MDC (VELCOM)	Belarus	Belarus

Source: Calculated from Averin (2004).

not been exhausted yet. Two companies dominate the Belarus mobile service market: MTS Belarus and Mobile Digital Communication (MDC). The third company, BelCel, keeps rather modest market share.

MDC operates under the VELCOM brand name. The company was set up in July 1998 as a joint venture between Belarus' state-controlled fixed-line monopolist Beltelecom (share of 31%), an armament and military equipment exporter Beltekhexport (share of 20%), and Cypriot SB Telecom Ltd (share of 49%).

MDC has base stations in all localities with population exceeding 10,000 residents. Its network covers 45% of national territory. During 2004, the company lost the leading market position it had enjoyed for more than five years. MDC market share decreased down to 45% in September 2004 from 56% in the beginning of the same year. Meanwhile, the company announced the plans to regain its leading position in 2005. To achieve this goal it is going to invest at least USD 65 million in new base stations aiming to cover 100% of urban population and 65% of the total Belarus territory.

BelCel was established in May 1993 as a Belarus-British joint venture. Currently, the company belongs to the Netherlands' CIB BV (50%), state telecom operator Minskaya Gorodskaya Telefonnaya Syet (30%), state company Minskobltelecom (3%), and Infobank (17%).

A new company, Belarus Telecommunication Network (BEST), was set up in November 2004 as a closed stock company jointly owned by state fixed-line monopolist Beltelecom and Agat, the state-run enterprise that manufactures, among other products, air defence computer control systems. BEST services have already launched in 2005.

MTS decided to enter the Belarus market via the establishing of a joint venture with a local company. It was long-distance operator Mezhdugorodnaya Svyaz. MTS Belarus began its operations in June 2002. Currently, MTS and Mezhdugorodnaya Svyaz hold respective stakes of 49% and 51% in the joint venture.

In 2004, MTS Belarus outran MDC and became the leader on national mobile market in terms of number of subscribers and the territory coverage. Access to company network is available on half of Belarus territory with 93% of urban population. These results were positively assessed by the Russian mother-company, which claimed that the more than two-year-long history of operations in Belarus appeared to be mutual beneficial for both partners.

Future prospects for MTS Belarus to a large extent depend upon the ability of the company to compete successfully both with MDC and BEST. The latter has really ambitious expansion plans to cover 60-70%

of the Belarus territory, including areas in which other existing companies have failed so far to establish their presence. While providing access to mobile services for low-income groups and rural residents these activities correspond to Belarus social regional development policy. Under the circumstances the company might rely on various forms of governmental support, in particular on state guarantees in obtaining loans.

Generally speaking, the political factor in a broad sense of the word is a very significant one for doing business in Belarus. This is particularly true for the telecommunication sector. In particular, the Belarus Government constantly reveals its serious concern regarding capital flight. Accordingly, both MTS and MDC were accused of withdrawing USD 20 million annually from Belarus. These accusations are largely groundless. In addition to their substantial contribution to wireless communication development in Belarus, MTS and MDC annually pay about USD 80 million in taxes (Sharova, 2004).

The attitude of the government is also crucial with respect to the plans of MTS to increase its stake in MTS Belarus up to 51% and afterwards seriously increase its investments. Previously the state had preferred to keep a larger interest in telecom companies. At the moment CIB BV with its 50% is the only exception. So far investments of the Russian partner into MTS Belarus have amounted to over USD 130 million since 2002. In the nearest future, MTS Belarus aims at improving the quality of services by investing substantially in the network development. In 2005, MTS Belarus plans to extend the installed capacity up to three million numbers. To achieve the goal the company is going to purchase state-of-art equipment and launch additional base stations in all regional centers.

Ukraine

Ukraine was the second target destination for MTS after Belarus. MTS entered this market just a few months later. In terms of population, Ukraine is the second largest market in the CIS (close to 50 million people). The population density is also relatively high–80 people per sq. km. After eight years of decline since the Soviet Union collapsed, Ukraine has been experiencing economic growth since 2000. GDP growth rate in Ukraine was even higher than in Russia and varied from 6% in 2000 to over 8% in 2003. At the same time, GDP per capita remains quite low (slightly over USD 1,000). This is far behind Russia and Belarus.

The Ukrainian mobile service sector is one of the dramatically growing industries in the country. The number of subscribers has been increasing rapidly (by 140% in 2001, 60% in 2002, and 80% in 2003). In September 2004, there were about 10 million mobile subscribers. According to mobile operators' forecasts, this figure could be more than 20 million by the end of 2005. The growth of the sector could be explained by two main reasons: low penetration rate of fixed lines (24%) and substantial price fall for mobile services. However, the penetration rate in the Ukrainian mobile sector is still quite low; it is just crossed 22%.

There are currently five licensed mobile operators in Ukraine. At the same time, the market in Ukraine is very similar to a duopoly model. The market is divided by two main players–Ukrainian Mobile Communications (UMC) and KyivStar GSM–which control together about 98% of the mobile sector. The remaining three mobile operators, Golden Telecom (GT), Ukrainian Radio Systems (URS, traded as WellCOM) and Digital Cellular Communications (DCC), do not significantly influence the market.

KyivStar GSM was founded in 1994 as a joint stock company. The company began its operations in 1997. It belongs to Norway's Telenor Mobile Communications (54%), the Ukrainian company Storm, and the local investor Omega (6%). The network of KyivStar covers the largest part of the Ukrainian territory and 87% of the country's population. The company plans substantial investments in order to improve quality of services.

MTS entered the Ukrainian mobile market in 2002 via purchasing the controlling interest of UMC (58% of shares). Step by step, the Russian company bought shares from the other owners. At the moment, MTS holds 99% of the Ukraine company directly and one per cent through its subsidiary PPT Telecom Kyiv. UMC was established in 1992 as a joint venture between national fixed-line operator Ukrtelecom (51%), TDC AS (Denmark), Deutsche Telekom (Germany), and Royal KPN NV (the Netherlands); each foreign company got 16% (Paul Budde Communication, 2002).

For the first eight years of operations UMC was the market leader. The trend changed in mid-2001, when the company faced network capacity problems and stopped accepting new subscribers for three months. KyivStar managed to use the opportunity to become a leader. At the end of 2001, the market share of UMC fell down from 55% to 46% (EMC, 2003).

When MTS decided to enter the Ukrainian mobile market, UMC was the second player. A brief history of the purchasing of UMC by the Russian company included several stages. In November 2002, MTS applied to the Ukrainian antimonopoly committee for permission to buy 58% of UMC and simultaneously to sign an option agreement to purchase the remaining 42% for some USD 140 million in 2003-2005. The first decision to sell UMC was taken by the Viktor Yushchenko government. In November 2002, MTS signed a USD 194 million contract to buy the first share holding by the end of the year. This controlling stake in its turn consisted of three parts. Ukrtelekom sold 25% of state ownership for approximately USD 85 million. Two packages of shares of Deutsche Telekom and KPN were sold for USD 55 million each. Since March 2003, MTS began to consolidate UMC in its financial statements.

Then MTS signed an option contract with Ukrtelekom to acquire a 26% share of UMC for almost USD 90 million. MTS took up the option in June 2003. MTS also signed an option contract to buy from TDC a 16% share of UMC for a price not less than USD 55 million. This share holding was actually sold in July 2003 for some USD 90 million. Being the only owner of UMC, MTS in April 2004 decided to transform the mobile operator from a limited liability enterprise into a closed joint stock company.

One could argue that the influence of MTS as an owner was rather positive for UMC. Managerial, financial and other types of input helped the latter to restore the leading position on the Ukrainian mobile market. Thus, the number of UMC subscribers as a subsidiary of MTS doubled in two years and the growth rate was higher then one of Kyivstar for the same period.

MTS also invests intensively in the network development. While UMC's total investments in ten years period amounted to over USD 450 million, MTS spent over USD 250 million on the UMC development in 2003 alone. According to estimates, the total stock of MTS investments in Ukraine amounts to USD 1.2 billion by the end of 2004. MTS actively co-operates with leading equipment suppliers (Alcatel and Siemens) to expand the UMC GSM network, optimize existing infrastructure, and accelerate development of next-generation products and services. As of September 2004, UMC's network covered over 80% of the country's territory and about 90% of the population. Having the status of the MTS subsidiary, UMC gets better access to foreign financial sources. Thus in 2004, UMC took over a USD 50 million loan from ING BHF-Bank and Commerzbank for financing the purchase of GSM equipment from Siemens.

However, despite certain success MTS faced some serious problems in Ukraine. They basically come from a high level of political risk in the country and ideas of re-privatization. In the case of UMC, the Ukrainian Prosecutor-General's Office (the PGO) in June 2004 claimed that the sale of Ukrtelecom share of the company to MTS was in breach of Ukraine's privatization laws, and therefore announced a re-privatization campaign. The initiators of the idea would like Ukrtelekom to regain 51% of UMC. In exchange, Ukraine would pay back to MTS the entire sum of money that it spent for the deal (over USD 170 million). At the same time, the Ukrainian Government does not examine any options that would allow MTS to get back its investments on the UMC development (BBC, 2004).

MTS managed to prove that it did not break the law and to win the trial in the court. The company also claimed that it was a victim of internal political disputes connected with the presidential election (EIU, 2004). Nevertheless, the Ukrainian Prosecutor-General said he would take another attempt to give the company back to Ukrtelecom. In addition to that, the case could be put on the agenda in connection with future plans to privatize Ukrtelecom. Since it sold its share to MTS, Ukrtelecom's value dropped down. The Ukrainian authorities wanted to increase as much as possible an attractiveness of future privatization tender. Due to the presidential election, these plans were postponed and it is not clear yet when the new government will come back to the issue.

Ukrainian authorities also blame UMC for low level of quality services. According to them, the mobile operator while attracting more clients does not care much about sufficient technical support. In particular, the company's subscribers suffered serious communication problems in Kyiv over August 31st-September 1st 2004. This infringes on the interests of consumers and may be considered as violation of the competition law. The Antimonopoly Committee forced the company to take urgent measures, threatening to take away its license. UMC announced it would compensate subscribers' losses. In addition to that it was actually forced to install five new switchboards to increase installed capacity and to avoid network congestion (Voltornist & Afanasiev, 2004).

The Antimonopoly Committee also criticizes UMC for keeping prices too high (at USD 0.13-0.21 per minute). In turn, MTS argues that the arrival of MTS on the Ukrainian market "*was a powerful jolt for its development: the level of penetration of cellular communications doubled. We are investing in the development of the country's telecommunications market and its infrastructure, which is beneficial both for the state and for consumers*" (BBC, 2004).

Despite the problems, MTS would like to stay at the Ukrainian market. It is going to pay extra attention to network development, to open new service centers (own and joint offices with the dealers), and to plan intensive marketing campaigns.

Uzbekistan

Uzbekistan is the third largest country in the CIS after Russia and Ukraine in terms of population. Almost 26 million inhabitants live there. The population density equals to over 50 persons per sq km. Similar to other CIS member-countries, Uzbekistan is a relatively fast developing market with GDP annual growth rate of about four per cent during the last seven years. At the same time, national living standards still remain pretty low with GDP per capita less than USD 400 in 2003.

Fixed telephone lines in Uzbekistan are obsolete, inadequate, and in serious need of modernization. The number of subscribers does not exceed two million people (less than 8% of population). As for mobile communication, the penetration rate currently does not exceed two per cent. At the same time, the Uzbek mobile market has started to grow really fast. For example, the number of mobile phone users in the country reached almost 470,000 in September of 2004 in comparison with 325,000 at the end of 2003. Under the circumstances economic agents assess prospects for the Uzbek mobile communications market as really promising, especially in the medium and long run.

Six companies currently run their operations on the Uzbek mobile communications market. Two of them keep dominant positions, namely Uzdunrobita with 250,000 subscribers and Daewoo Unitel with over 100,000 subscribers. The others are far behind the leaders.

Daewoo Unitel, launched in 1997, is the second largest GSM network operator in Uzbekistan with a market share of 23%. Its network covers major densely populated areas of the country. In autumn of 2004, Daewoo International sold the company for USD 75 million to a consortium of Germanos SA (the largest telecom equipment company in Greece), EBRD, and Global Finance (Greek private equity and venture capital firm that manages the Black Sea Fund, in which the EBRD is an investor). Germanos SA decided to participate in this acquisition taking under consideration favorable prospects for the market under review as well as a commitment to vertical integration strategy. On the other hand, having EBRD as one of the shareholders, Daewoo Unitel might have a better access to financial resources. This would allow the company to develop and modernize its network. The activities under review should be mostly focused on expanding the geographic coverage and product range. The ultimate goal is to make mobile services more affordable in economic terms and hence to capture the lower income segment of the population.

MTS began its expansion towards Uzbekistan through the acquisition of Uzdunrobita, the leading mobile service company functioning in the country, which controlled approximately a half of the market. The deal immediately put MTC into the position of a leading player in the market. In August 2004, MTS purchased three-quarters of Uzdunrobita for some USD 120 million from two private companies. The agreement also included an option to acquire the remaining quarter for not less than USD 40 million. In this case MTS will be the only owner of the company. The deal requires the permission of national regulators both in Russia and Uzbekistan, as well as approval of the MTS board of directors, before it can be completed. MTS plans to participate in further development of Uzdunrobita projects aimed at improving the quality of its services.

The acquisition of Uzdunrobita was an expensive one for MTS. Indeed, the company already paid almost USD 500 per each subscriber it got. At the moment it looks like an open question whether MTS will manage to recoup its investments quickly enough and to gain sufficient experience for future market expansion towards other countries.

Turkmenistan

Turkmenistan became only recently the target country of MTS foreign market extension. The population of Turkmenistan is not as large as in other CIS countries where MTS operates (5 million people). The population density is relatively low (10 people per sq. km). The Turkmen economy has been demonstrating the highest GDP growth in the CIS region in the last several years (some 17% in 1999, 20% in 2002, 17% in 2003). In terms of GDP per capita, the country has the fourth highest rating in the CIS (over USD 1200 in 2003). The penetration of mobile communication services does not exceed one per cent–the lowest level in the CIS region. Analysts regarded Turkmenistan as a great potential market for telecommunications.

By the beginning of 2005, the USA-based American Barash Communication Technologies Inc. (BCTI) was the only mobile communication company in Turkmenistan. BCTI owns the entire range of frequencies required to establish GSM and 3G networks: 900 MHz, 1,800 Mhz, 1,900

MHz and others. The only other mobile communication license belongs to the Turkmen Ministry of Telecommunications.

Similar to its previous experience in Uzbekistan, MTS decided to enter the Turkmen market by purchasing the leader. At the moment, the deal valued for USD 55 million is at the final stage, although MTS has not confirmed it yet. If the purchase takes place, it would be the highest per-subscriber price ever paid by a Russian mobile company for cellular assets. Despite direct commercial considerations, experts treat the contract as a very important one from the political point of view. For the first time in the post-Soviet history, a Russian telecom company could get the position of the monopolist on the foreign market.

Kazakhstan

The mobile penetration level in Kazakhstan slightly exceeds 13%; that is much less than in Russia. To date, the market is still in its infancy. That mainly results from the vast territory of the country in combination with inadequate infrastructure. At the same time, that provides good growth opportunities. The number of mobile subscribers increased more than 13-fold since 2000. Annual growth in 2004 slowed down in comparison with previous years, but 86% still looked impressive and attractive for newcomers.

Competition on the national market is high compared to that in Uzbekistan and Turkmenistan. The general situation resembles the Ukrainian model. There are two obvious leaders (GSM-Kazakhstan and KaR-Tel) as well as two smaller companies.

GSM-Kazakhstan (works with two trademarks, K-cell and Active) today holds almost three-quarters of the Kazakh telecom market. The total number of its subscribers amounts to over one million as of August 2004. The company has two main owners: 51% of its stock belongs to the Dutch company Fintur Holdings B.V. (owned by Scandinavian TeliaSonera and Turkish Turkcell) and 49% are the property of nationally-based Kazakhtelecom.

Kazakhstan's second largest mobile operator, KaR-Tel (works with two trademarks K-Mobile and Excess), has approximately 600,000 registered subscribers at the end of August 2004, and its market share is about 25%. Initially, KaR-Tel was a Kazakh-Turkish joint venture but the Kazakh side accused its two Turkish partners in non-observance of obligations and took their shares back through the court. In August 2004, Kazakh owners organized a tender for KaR-Tel. Eight companies participated in the tender; among them were the Russian mobile operators MTS and VimpelCom. The latter won the tender and purchased whole KaR-Tel from the Kazakh parent company for USD 350 million and simultaneously took a burden of KaR-Tel's huge debt (Yevstigneyeva, 2004).

The price of the deal was pretty high, but VimpelCom perceives the Kazakh mobile market as very important for its international expansion, as it was the first foreign market for the company. VimpelCom had previously focused on the rapid growth of its network towards the Russian regions. Moreover, buying a local operator may be the only path to international expansion in Kazakhstan. Earlier in February 2004, VimpelCom tried and failed to win a tender for Kazakhstan's third GSM license. The aim of the company in Kazakhstan for the coming years is reportedly to increase mobile penetration in urban areas to 70% (more than half of the Kazakh population lives in urban areas).

So far Kazakhstan is the only CIS market where MTS has tried and failed to enter. On the other hand, relatively low penetration level and importance of Kazakhstan as a large and rapidly developing market is a challenge for the leader of Russian telecom. Deepening of economic integration between Russia and Kazakhstan may enhance the penetration of the Russian companies to the neighboring country, and many of them are corporate clients of MTS. That may create an additional incentive for the company to repeat its attempts to enter the Kazakh market.

Other CIS Countries

Armenia, Azerbaijan, Georgia, Kyrgyzstan, Moldova and Tajikistan have much in common and generally belong to MTS' target markets in the CIS. Under the circumstances one might argue that the company sooner or later will try to enter them within the framework of its further internationalization efforts.

All the aforementioned countries are relatively small in terms of population (the smallest one–Armenia–has only three million inhabitants) and have low living standards (Tajikistan has the lowest income level in the CIS as well as one of the lowest in the world). Nevertheless, development of the telecom sector in these countries varies. For example, Tajikistan, Kyrgyzstan and Armenia are evident outsiders among the CIS countries in terms of such indicators as subscriber base and penetration level, which do not exceed five per cent.

Azerbaijan might be perceived as a relatively promising target. However, its market is mostly closed and highly monopolized. Just two mobile operators control the market. Azercell Telecom is a joint venture holding almost 70% of the national market of mobile communications in Azerbaijan. The company, founded in 1996, belongs to the state (51%) and to a foreign investor, Fintur Holding B.V. (49%). Bakcell was the first privatized mobile operator in Azerbaijan, which initially had been partly state owned, but later became fully private. Today this operator belongs to an Israel company, GTIB-96. Bakcell holds 30% of the Azerbaijan telecom market.

State officials express doubt about the intentions of Russian companies (first of all MTS and Rostelecom) to enter the market. They argue that the Azerbaijan telecom market currently does not need a third operator due to drawbacks in the licensing system. Moreover, if such an opportunity arises, the state could look at more appealing bids than MTS for the third operator. At any rate, MTS has not still made any official offer to the Azerbaijan telecom regulating authorities.

Georgia and Moldova are both markets with rather high competition (penetration level equals to 18% and 15% correspondingly) and the presence of national and foreign telecom companies (from the USA, the EU, and Turkey). But experts assess these markets as having relatively low growth potential. Territorial conflicts still split the territories of these states. For example, Moldova still has two separate communication networks: one for the Dniester Moldovan Republic, and one for the rest of the country. The same problems exist in Georgia.

The Armenian market was monopolized for a long period, and the only operator was ArmenTel. This monopoly had a negative impact on the overall development of mobile communication in the country. In particular, penetration level equals to some five per cent only. In November 2004, the Armenian Government deprived ArmenTel of the exclusive right for GSM and satellite communication services. In the same month a second mobile operator, nationally-based K-Telekom, appeared on the market. This recent reform gave a green light to foreign companies (Russian as well) interested in entering the Armenian market.

Kyrgyzstan has one of the lowest income levels within the CIS (GDP per capita in 2003 was less than USD 350). Nevertheless, low penetration rate (5%) presumes high growth potential. There are two mobile operators on the market, but there is still enough space for the newcomers, and the current subscriber base growth is very high. So, the Kyrgyz market of mobile communication is rather interesting for the Russian companies. Experts suppose that VimpelCom and MegaFon may take certain efforts to enter this market in the nearest future, and that is an obvious challenge for MTS.

Tajikistan, the poorest among the CIS countries, experienced the highest market growth rates in the alliance (almost 640 from September 2003 till September 2004). That fact already attracted one leading Russian operator, MegaFon, which entered the Tajik market in 2001 by acquiring 75% of local operator TT Mobile. Besides, there are three other telecom companies on the market. Taking into account that for MegaFon Tajikistan is the only foreign market, one can argue that MTS may not concentrate on expanding to this country, at least in the short run.

CONCLUSIONS

In each CIS country where MTS operates one could observe sustainable mobile market growth. This growth could be explained by two main reasons: an urgent need for modern communication tools on the one hand, and aggressive marketing campaigns of mobile service providers on the other hand.

Entry modes for MTS were predetermined by technological and regulatory considerations. As for target markets, they largely resulted from historical and cultural traditions, common infrastructure network, similar business practices, and development of re-integration process within the framework of the CIS. MTS started the internationalization process in 2002 and since then entered several markets in the region gradually increasing its experience. One could argue that MTS would use its knowledge and existing positions as the platform for future expansion to other CIS countries.

Due to various types of similarities between Russia and its neighbors MTS may better understand market environment in the region in comparison with Western counterparts, and therefore use this understanding as its competitive advantage. At the same time, the main threats would most probably come not from national telecom service suppliers, but from large Western telecoms with huge financial recourses.

Regarding regulatory issues, it is necessary to mention that without the political will of the national authorities MTS could not get access to their privatization processes. In addition to that, due to the high level of monopolization in most of the countries under review, in order to be successful MTS should establish a good relationship with local anti-monopoly agencies.

MTS positions itself as an international company and the leading mobile service provider in Russia and the CIS countries. Hence, in three cases (out of four) it entered foreign countries by purchasing the most successful national mobile companies with prominent market shares. Only in Belarus it made greenfield investments and then the company did its best to gain the leading position in the local telecom sector.

NOTE

1. Estimations for the end of 2004.

REFERENCES

Averin Sergei & Fomina Ekaterina (2005). Obzor rinka sotovoi svjazi Ukraini. Itogi 2004. *Sotovik.* http://www.sotovik.ru/analyt/sng/ukrain/ukrain_226.html.

Averin Sergei &Fomina Ekaterina (2005). Obzor rinka sotovoi svjazi stran SNG i Baltii. Itogi 2004. *Sotovik.* http://www.sotovik.ru/analyt/russia/russia2004/index_230.html.

Averin Sergei (2004). Obzor rinka sotovoi svjazi stran SNG i Baltii. Itogi 3Q2004. *Sotovik.* http://www.sotovik.ru/analyt/russia/russia2004/index_212.htm.

BBC Monitoring (2004) Web site looks at moves to cancel sale of Ukrainian mobile phone company. *BBC*, June 23, 2004. http://www.monitor.bbc.co.uk.

CIT (2003). *Datafile of Eastern European Telecommunications.* CIT Publications Limited, September, 2003, p. Ukr_1-Ukr_ F4.

Efimova Elena, Vadim Kapustkin & Sergei Sutyrin (1996). Comparative analysis of foreign entry strategies of western and CIS firms in each other markets. Choice and Management of Entry Strategies in International Business. *Proceedings of the University of Vaasa*, Jorma Larimo and Tuija Mainela (eds.). Vaasa.

EIU (2004). *Ukraine will seek to annul 2002 deal with MTS.* The Economist Intelligence Unit Research report, June 24, 2004. http://www.eiu.com.

EMC (2003). *European Mobile Communications Report.* Issue 176, 2003. http://www.emc-database.com.

EMC (2004). *European Mobile Communications Report.* Issue 186, 2004. http://www.emc-database.com.

Gaidar Egor (2005). Postsovietskaya Istoria. *Vedomosti.* Issue No. 8 (1289). Moscow.

Intergovernmental Statistical Committee of the CIS Countries (2004). *Economic Development of the CIS Countries.* Report. http://www.cisstat.com.

Johansson, Jan. & Vahlne, J.-E. (1990). The Mechanism of Internationalization. *International Marketing Review*, 7 (4): 11-24.

J'son & Partners (2004). *Cellular Communication in Russia Information Bulletin.* J'son & Partners Management Consultancy. http://www.json.ru.

Liuhto Kari (ed.). (2001) *East Goes West–The Internationalization of Eastern Enterprises* (2001). Lappeenranta University of Technology, Lappeenranta.

McMillan Carl H. (1996). *Foreign Investment in Russia: Soviet Legacies and Post-Soviet Prospects. Foreign Investment in Russia and Other Soviet Successor States*. Ed. by Artisien-Maksimenko P., Adjubei Y. London, 1996.

Paul Budde Communication (2002) *Telecoms in Russia, Belarus, Moldova and Ukraine 2003*. Paul Budde Communication, pp. 1-54 http://www.budde.com.au/publications/annual/eastern europe/russia-belarus-moldova-ukraine.html.

Paul Budde Communication (2004). *South Asian Telecoms, Mobile and Broadband Market reports*. http://www.budde.com.au/publications/annual/asia/south-asian-market-summary.html.

Sharova Yuliya (2004). State-Run Third GSM Operator to be Established for Taxpayers' Money, *BelaPAN Economic Review*, 25.10.04. http://www.belapan.com.

Vahtra Peeter, Liuhto Kari (2004). Expansion or Exodus?–Foreign Operations of the Russia's Largest Corporations. *Pan-European Institute Electronic Publications*. 8/2004. http://www.tukkk.fi.

Voltornist Andriy & Afanasiev Andrew (2004). Ukraine Mobile: Subscribers Prefer to Prepay, *IntelliNews Publication*, September 20, 2004, ISI Emerging Markets. http:// www.securities.com.

Welch Lawrence & Luostarinen Reijo (1993). Inward-Outward Connections in Internationalisation. *Journal of International Marketing*. Vol. 1, Issue 1. pp. 44-56.

World Bank (2005). *World Development Report*. World Bank Group, http://worldbank.org.

WTO (2005). *World Trade Report*, World Trade Organisation, http://www.wto.org

Yevstigneyeva Tatyana (2004). Russian Mobile Expansion to Strengthen Kazakh Market, *IntelliNews Publication*, September 6, 2004, ISI Emerging Markets. http://www.securities.com.

Numerous articles in various business reviews and Internet sources, information obtained from the companies under review.

Index

In this index, page numbers in *italics* designate figures; page numbers followed by the letter "t" designate tables.

